Management Guidelines for World Cultural Heritage Sites

Bernard M. Feilden and Jukka Jokilehto

ICCROM

Second Edition
Rome, 1998

ISBN 92-9077-150-X

© 1998 ICCROM

ICCROM – International Centre for the Study of the
Preservation and Restoration of Cultural Property
Via di San Michele 13
I-00153 Rome RM, Italy

E-mail: iccrom@iccrom.org

Printed in Italy
by OGRARO

Style editing/typesetting/layout
Cynthia Rockwell with Thorgeir Lawrence

Cover design by Studio *PAGE*

CONTENTS

4 MANAGEMENT OF WORLD HERITAGE SITES

5 MANAGEMENT BY RESOURCE PROJECTS

6 MAINTENANCE PROGRAMME

PREFACE TO THE SECOND EDITION

These management guidelines were first published by ICCROM in English in 1993. Providing 'in a nutshell' some of the most pertinent principles in the conservation and management of cultural heritage, the guidelines have met with an encouraging response, as shown by the ongoing demand for translations in various languages. These include a French edition published by ICCROM in 1996 and a Spanish edition published in Colombia in 1995. Translations into Chinese, Thai, Persian, Polish, German, Russian and Lithuanian are being published as well.

Considering the variety of values and the complexity of issues related to safeguarding cultural heritage in different countries, it will be obvious to the reader that one book can hardly cope with all situations. These guidelines, therefore, should be conceived as a general framework, and should be properly interpreted in the particular situations arising in each specific case.

The present edition is proposed with some minor corrections compared to the original 1993 edition. Some of these consist of updating the administrative guidelines according to the latest available edition of the *Operational Guidelines* of the UNESCO World Heritage Committee (February 1997). Such official documents are frequently revised, so it is advisable to verify whether further modifications have been made. New versions can be obtained either from the World Heritage Centre at UNESCO or by consulting the Home Page of UNESCO World Heritage. Other corrections result from clarifications of the original text, such as the definition of the concept of 'value,' as well as the issue of 'authenticity' in relation to modern conservation, revised following the outcome of the Nara meeting in 1994. Some new appendices have also been added.

Bernard Feilden and *Jukka Jokilehto*
May 1998

This set of guidelines originated from a joint meeting organized in Rome by the International Centre for the Study of the Preservation and the Restoration of Cultural Property (ICCROM) and the International Council on Monuments and Sites (ICOMOS), under the auspices of the Cultural Heritage Division of UNESCO in April 1983.

From their wide range of experience, the following experts contributed to the formulation of these guidelines:

BOURKE, Max	Australia
DIMACOPOULOS, Jordan	Greece
FEILDEN, Sir Bernard	United Kingdom
JOKILEHTO, Jukka	ICCROM
LEBLANC, François	Canada
MILLER, Hugh	USA
MOJSILOVIC-POPOVIC, Svetlana	Yugoslavia
MTURI, Amini A.	Tanzania
QUDSI, Adli	Syria

An outline of the contents was prepared by the working party, and Sir Bernard Feilden was entrusted with the task of writing the text. The Countryside Commission of the UK, Mr Andrew Thornburn and Dr Jukka Jokilehto helped in producing a revised draft incorporating the constructive comments of all the members of the original committee. The draft was then circulated to several conservation experts and managers in different countries, and their comments were also taken into consideration. The final text was prepared jointly by Bernard Feilden and Jukka Jokilehto, with editorial assistance from Susan Bronson and Barrett Kennedy.

Other manuals and guidelines have been initiated in the meantime, and the present publication should be seen as an integral part of a wider context. In particular, another manual now available is *Risk Preparedness: A Management Manual for World Cultural Heritage,* by Herb Stovel, former Secretary-General of ICOMOS.

Background

For those States Parties to the UNESCO World Heritage Convention that lack a developed system for the protection of their cultural heritage, the system proposed in these guidelines may seem complicated. The greatest challenge is to secure sufficient specialist personnel for the care and protection of their heritage. However, the proposed system is conceived to be followed in its broad outlines and used as a framework to accommodate the systems of each State Party as those systems develop. Often, developing countries are rich in the craft resources that are a 'living cultural heritage' and vital for the conservation of sites.

When a site is inscribed on the World Heritage List, it is recognised as having outstanding universal value, being one of about 500 such sites in the whole world. It is found that only a few States Parties (countries) have adjusted their administrative and town planning procedures, to recognise this new and enhanced status of a site, which also brings challenges from tourism and new development. The designation of buffer zones is an urgent priority.

The States Parties should have a positive attitude to World Heritage, with commitment to the principles, which means that all concerned should know and apply these principles, including community involvement – a shared heritage with shared responsibility.

In view of the immense variety in World Heritage sites, ranging from prehistoric paintings to cities such as Rome, the authors have to outline principles, rather than give recipes for action.

Management planning should focus on values, using them as an explicit basis for decision making.

This booklet has already been translated into several languages. It is suggested that it would assist site managers and staff if they can read it in their own tongue.

Who has the day-to-day, hour-by-hour responsibility for the management of a World Cultural Heritage site? The site may be chock-a-block with visitors, but who is responsible? There may be a Director-General, but, unless he or she has delegated adequate authority, no local person is in effective charge. Without local management control, anything can happen. The preventive actions needed to protect cultural heritage must be taken by specially trained staff who understand its significance.

These guidelines are written for all those concerned with a World Heritage site, but are applicable to other sites preserved for their cultural values. The aim is to help site management staff to become alert and self-sufficient, with adequate resources and active support from their central government. Since conservation is an essential part of the management process, the theory guiding conservation actions must be understood and used by the multidisciplinary management team.

The designation of a site as World Heritage implies changes. Increased numbers of visitors demand new facilities and bring in more traders. Shops that encroach on the site in a few days may take years to remove, even if their presence is totally illegal. A government may seek to enhance its site by over-restoration. The landscape and setting of the site may be damaged by intrusive development, such as engineering works or mineral extraction, and so on. Management should focus on risk assessment.

Management is essential, and can only be exercised at the site. What are the responsibilities of a site manager? A visitor has a serious accident: someone has to deal with it. A school party arrives unexpectedly without having booked, it is raining heavily and there is no shelter. There has even been a case where a dry riverbed flooded and a party was swept away by a sudden storm. Continuous erosion of the site causes floors with inscriptions to become worn. Even the rocks of the Acropolis need protection. Crowding of visitors leads to frustration and this may promote vandalism. Litter has to be cleared, paths repaired, plants protected and the needs of wild animals respected. The site manager has constantly to monitor security and be on guard against arson. All this strain on the management is to enable the citizens of the world to enjoy their cultural heritage. These citizens should be encouraged to report to the World Heritage Centre.

Politicians and administrators will be primarily interested in the principles, the Director-General in the policy, and the staff in the practicalities of site management. Conservation theory should guide all actions. The site manager is caught between daily problems and the larger issues imposed by supervisors, who have an eye on the budget but for whom the prime need is to conserve the World Heritage site.

The enjoyment of our heritage depends upon its conservation. These guidelines aim to assist site managers to fulfil this role with the support of a commission of experts, by understanding *what it is that makes the site significant* and protecting it from the numerous threats to which it is exposed.

World Heritage demonstrates that the industry, craftsmanship, love and care of past civilizations were given to make their surroundings meaningful. This should never cease to fill us with wonder. The past can speak to us and help us realize where we are going in the future.

Bernard Feilden and *Jukka Jokilehto*
May 1998

Chapter 1

SUMMARY OF THE GUIDING PRINCIPLES

1.1 OBJECTIVES

❑ *These* **Management Guidelines** *are intended to provide advice and suggestions for implementing the intentions of the World Heritage Convention.*

They contain information which will be useful for all States Parties to the UNESCO *Convention Concerning the Protection of the World Cultural and Natural Heritage*. The State Party will have already designated World Heritage sites in accordance with conventions, guidelines and forms prescribed by UNESCO.[1]

Management techniques can be applied at any level of technical sophistication and can be used to raise levels of technical competence.

❑ *Priority should be given to establishing the framework for management.*

❑ *All proposed activities must be based on interdisciplinary collaboration using conservation theory to evaluate alternative proposals.*

❑ *The management plan will consist of several interrelated resource project plans.*

Each State Party should apply the principles given in these guidelines according to the degree of sophistication in management that can be made efficient and effective. If the basic framework of actions suggested in these guidelines is followed initially, greater sophistication can be achieved in subsequent stages, when it is perceived to be necessary and when the required professionals are available.

Actions to implement the management of World Heritage sites should be based upon the traditions and legislation of the State Party, which should review its legislation and update it if necessary.

---

1   Updated information on the World Heritage Convention and related issues can be found on the Internet at: <http://www.unesco.org:80/whc/>. In particular the UNESCO Conventions should be consulted, as these guidelines are based on the assumption that the State Party adheres to and implements the said Conventions. The Recommendations of UNESCO also provide complementary guidelines for implementation of conservation policies. In addition to the list of references given in the last chapter, selected bibliographies relating to the management of historic areas, buildings and sites may be requested from ICCROM in Rome, Italy, or from the Conservation Information Network (CIN) in Ottawa, Canada.

The management of a World Heritage site is based on the detailed analysis of its significance as identified during the nomination procedure. Management includes the following:

- ensuring that all site staff understand the cultural values to be preserved in the site;
- providing specific guidelines based upon the statement of significance of the site;
- making a complete inventory of all the cultural resources within the site;
- arranging for regular inspections and formal reports by professionals with suitable qualifications and experience;
- drafting a strategic maintenance plan leading to the formulation of resource projects which are incorporated into an annual work programme according to their priority; and
- respecting, in all work, the ethics of conservation, the established international recommendations of UNESCO, and guidelines such as the Venice Charter.

1.2   DOCUMENTATION

All pertinent published literature relating to the site should be collected, catalogued and made accessible. The statement of significance should take this material into account. If this has not been done, the omission should be rectified as a matter of urgency.

Management of the site should be based on the State Party's legislation controlling land use, but additional protection may have to be applied, particularly to the area surrounding the site. The inventory should include all buildings and, where appropriate, their contents as well as the townscape and landscape resources within the site.

1.3   WORK PLANS

Long-term (5-30+ years), medium-term (<5 years), and annual work plans are the basis of management planning, programming and budgeting. Annual programmes may consist of a number of related projects which can be brought forward for approval by stages.

Management should be organized by resource projects according to a standard methodology. Since programming will depend on both the capacity of the staff and the budget, resource projects must be identified in advance and implemented in order of priority.

Research activities will require planning, coordinating and management under a separate committee; a brief outline should be attached as an appendix to the management plan. Town planning studies form part of the management plan, being integrated on the basis of regular inspections.

One aim of conservation is to **not** lower living standards of the occupants of historic areas, so rehabilitation guided by suitable standards and guidelines may be necessary.

1.4   PREVENTIVE MAINTENANCE

A preventive maintenance strategy should be developed, based upon a multidisciplinary approach. When practical, alternative courses have been examined, conservation theory should be used to evaluate the prescription to be adopted.

Maintenance includes all practical and technical measures that are needed to keep the site in condition at a standard that permits enjoyment of the cultural resource without damage. It is a continuous process. Frequencies of action should be defined based upon professional input and special training of craftspersons. Monitoring of the maintenance programme is necessary.

Special precautions may be needed against vandalism, theft, fire, floods and earthquakes.

1.5   PERSONNEL

Suitable experts must be selected to advise on the work plan and to assist in its execution. The plan should start with a statement of management philosophy, couched in terms all **site** staff can appreciate. Staffing requirements must be assessed, and key staff should be appointed first. Staffing and personnel are discussed in Chapter 7.

1.6   SITE COMMISSION

The establishment of a Site Commission is recommended.

The Site Commission should act as a guardian of the World Heritage site. Its primary duty is to conserve and manage the site. The form of the Site Commission should be dictated by practical considerations, and its name – be it task force, agency, commission, etc. – should fit into the national administrative pattern. If sufficiently close geographically, several small World Heritage sites with similar problems could come under one Commission (e.g., within the State Party's archaeological organization). Certain bodies, such as committees of city councils, could act as Site Commissions.

It is desirable that the Site Commission have a budget for providing general information, promoting public awareness and accommodating school education, and that the mass media and other channels of communication be used to publicize the site worldwide. The production of guidebooks merits serious consideration. Visitor and community services ought to be provided, but the maximum capacity of the site should not be exceeded, and security and protection may have to be provided. The policy on admission fees needs study. Training and licensing of guides is usually the responsibility of the Site Commission.

Economics will control much of the Site Commission's activities. Although depending in a large part on a state grant for site **preservation** and **research** studies, the commission should be allowed to raise money from tourists in order to **develop** the site and so increase visitor enjoyment, as well as defraying some costs. Annual budgeting should be established within a framework of governmental finance, with powers to carry fiscal allocations forward from one year to the next. Budgeting should be under standardized headings.

Chapter 2

GENERAL POLICY OF THE CONVENTION

2.1 THE WORLD HERITAGE COMMITTEE

The *Convention Concerning the Protection of the World Cultural and Natural Heritage* is one of the three UNESCO Conventions related to cultural heritage,[1] and was adopted by the General Conference of UNESCO at its seventeenth session in Paris on 16 November 1972. As of 28 October 1997, 152 states had deposited an instrument of ratification, acceptance or accession to this Convention.

The Convention is managed by the **World Heritage Committee** assisted by the UNESCO Secretariat, the World Heritage Centre. Decisions are prepared for the Committee by the **World Heritage Bureau**, which consists of a chair, vice-chairs and a rapporteur. The Committee, which consists of representatives of States Parties, generally meets once a year. The three essential functions of the Committee are:

- to identify, on the basis of nominations submitted by States Parties, cultural and natural properties of outstanding universal value which are to be protected under the Convention, and to list those properties on the **World Heritage List**;
- to decide which properties on the World Heritage List are to be inscribed on the **List of World Heritage in Danger** (i.e., properties on the World Heritage List that are threatened and would require major operations for their conservation; generally a request for assistance is required); and
- to determine in what way and under what conditions the resources in the **World Heritage Fund** can most advantageously be used to assist States Parties in the protection of their properties of outstanding universal value.

2.2 OPERATIONAL GUIDELINES

The *Operational Guidelines for the Implementation of the World Heritage Convention* (hereinafter simply referred to as the *Operational Guidelines*), first written in 1977 and periodically revised,[2] were prepared for the purpose of informing States Parties to the Convention of the principles that guide the work of

---

1   The others are: *Convention for the Protection of Cultural Property in the Event of Armed Conflict* (the Hague Convention), adopted in 1954, and *Convention on the Means of Prohibiting and Preventing the Illicit Import, Export and Transfer of Ownership of Cultural Property*, of 1970.

2   These *Management Guidelines* reflect all such revisions up to and including the changes to the *Operational Guidelines* as adopted by the 16th Session of the World Heritage Committee in Merida, Mexico, December 1996 (WHC-97-2, February 1997).

the Committee in establishing the World Heritage List and the List of World Heritage in Danger, as well as in granting international assistance under the World Heritage Fund. The *Operational Guidelines* are considered a working tool, and may be edited and revised by the World Heritage Committee according to local needs in accordance with the policies defined for the Convention by the Committee.

2.3   NOMINATION TO THE WORLD HERITAGE LIST

One of the principal aims of the World Heritage Convention is to identify specific heritage sites, cultural or natural, to be nominated to the World Heritage List. To be eligible, the cultural heritage should be of outstanding universal value; the specific criteria for nomination to the World Heritage List are defined in the *Operational Guidelines* (Section C., par. 23-34) and refer to three categories of World Heritage sites: (a) monuments, groups of buildings and sites; (b) groups of urban buildings; and (c) cultural landscapes.

The criteria for category (a) sites are that they must:

(a) (i) represent a masterpiece of human creative genius; or

     (ii) exhibit an important interchange of human values, over a span of time or within a cultural area of the world, on developments in architecture, monumental arts, town-planning or landscape design; or

     (iii) bear a unique or at least exceptional testimony to a cultural tradition or to a civilization which is living or has disappeared; or

     (iv) be an outstanding example of a type of building or architectural ensemble or landscape which illustrates (a) significant stage(s) in human history; or

     (v) be an outstanding example of traditional human settlement or land-use which is representative of a culture (or cultures), especially when it has become vulnerable under the impact of irreversible change; or

     (vi) be directly or tangibly associated with events or living traditions, with ideas, or with beliefs, with artistic and literary works of outstanding universal significance (the Committee considers that this criterion should justify inclusion in the List only in exceptional circumstances or in conjunction with other criteria cultural or natural);

In addition, a World Heritage site must:

(b) (i) meet the test of authenticity in design, material, workmanship or setting and in the case of cultural landscapes their distinctive character and components (the Committee stressed that reconstruction is only acceptable if it is carried out on the basis of complete and detailed documentation on the original and to no extent on conjecture).

(ii) have adequate legal protection and/orcontractural and/or traditional protection and management mechanisms to ensure the conservation of the
nominated cultural property or cultural landscapes. The existence of
protective legislation at the national, provincial and municipal level or
well-established traditional protection and/or management mechanisms
is therefore essential and must be stated clearly on the nomination form.
Assurances of the effective implementation of these laws and/or management mechanisms are also expected. Furthermore, in order to preserve the integrity of cultural sites, particularly those open to large
numbers of visitors, the State Party concerned should be able to provide
evidence of suitable administrative arrangements to cover the management of the property, its conservation and its accessibility to the public.

Category (b) covers **groups of urban buildings**, and refers mainly to historic
towns.[3] These are classified into three types (par. 27):

(i) towns which are no longer inhabited but which provide unchanged
archaeological evidence of the past; these generally satisfy the criterion
of authenticity and their state of conservation can be relatively easily
controlled;

(ii) historic towns which are still inhabited and which, by their very nature,
have developed and will continue to develop under the influence of
socio-economic and cultural change, a situation that renders the assessment of their authenticity more difficult and any conservation policy
more problematical;

(iii) new towns of the twentieth century which paradoxically have something
in common with both the aforementioned categories: while their original
urban organization is clearly recognizable and their authenticity is unde-
niable, their future is unclear because their development is largely
uncontrollable.

The *Operational Guidelines* define the criteria for the nomination of historic towns
as follows (par. 29):

> To qualify for inclusion, towns should compel recognition because of
> their architectural interest and should not be considered only on the
> intellectual grounds of the role they may have played in the past or
> their value as historical symbols under criterion (vi) for the inclusion
> of cultural properties in the World Heritage List. To be eligible for
> inclusion in the List, the spatial organization, structure, materials,
> forms and, where possible, functions of a group of buildings should
> essentially reflect the civilization or succession of civilizations which
> have prompted the nomination of the property.

---

3 The term *towns* is used generically throughout these *Management Guidelines* to also include cities
and other urban sites.

The historic towns that are nominated can fall into several categories depending on their extent, from including the entire historic town (such as Rome) to including only a significant area within the historic town area (such as the Meidan-e-Shah square in Isfahan) or taking a selection of significant monuments that document specific features in the town's history. In all cases, however, **an integrated approach** is necessary because, first, these elements are an integral part of their urban context, even if representing a different historical period, and, second, their conservation is in most cases directly dependent on the management of their physical and socio-economic context.

Category (c), identified since 1992, covers cultural landscapes which are eligible under three main categories (*Operational Guidelines*, par. 39):

(i) landscape designed and created intentionally by man (e.g., garden, parkland);

(ii) organically evolved landscape resulting from an initial social, economic, administrative, and/or religious imperative (relict or fossil landscapes, continuing landscapes);

(iii) the associative cultural landscape – justifiable by virtue of powerful religious, artistic or cultural associations or natural element.

The question of the **test of authenticity** should be understood in this context as relating to historic buildings, whereas for cultural landscapes, their distinctive character and components must be taken into consideration.

The word *site* will be used to refer to all the categories contained in the definitions given above. In some cases, however, both cultural and natural heritage resources are found together. The methodology of management by resource projects is remarkably similar in both cases. The criteria for the inclusion of natural properties in the World Heritage List are defined in section D (par. 43-45) of the *Operational Guidelines*.

2.4   GLOBAL STRATEGY

In 1990, the World Heritage Committee initiated a project, called the **Global Study**, aimed at establishing an overall framework of the world's cultural heritage and providing a reference for future nominations. In 1994, this project was renamed **Global Strategy**, conceived as a conceptual framework devised to ensure the representativeness and credibility of the World Heritage List, and subsequently enlarged to cover natural heritage as well. The strategy foresees the organization of regional and thematic meetings, such as those on cultural landscapes of outstanding universal value (von Droste *et al* 1995) and meetings on authenticity (Larson and Marstein 1994, Larson 1995). This ongoing project is being carried out in collaboration with the competent authorities and specialists in States Parties, ICOMOS and ICCROM.

2.5 OBJECTIVES OF PROTECTION AND CONSERVATION

The World Heritage Convention can be seen in the more general context of international collaboration, also taking into account the other UNESCO Conventions and Recommendations (see list in appendix), and the following in particular: Recommendation concerning the Protection, at National Level, of the Cultural and Natural Heritage (1972), and Recommendation concerning the Safeguarding and Contemporary Role of Historic Areas (1976). Considering the objectives of protection and conservation of World Heritage properties, specific indications are provided in Section II (art. 4-7) of the Convention, which deals with *National Protection and International Protection of the Cultural and Natural Heritage*. The following principles on measures for protection (art. 5) are particularly relevant to the *Management Guidelines* being expressed in this publication.

To ensure that effective and active measures are taken for the protection, conservation and presentation of the cultural and natural heritage situated on its territory, each State Party to this Convention shall endeavour, in so far as is possible, and as appropriate for each country:

- to adopt a general policy which aims to give the cultural and natural heritage a function in the life of the community and to integrate the protection of that heritage into comprehensive planning programmes;
- to set up within its territories, where such services do not exist, one or more services for the protection, conservation and presentation of the cultural and natural heritage with an appropriate staff and possessing the means to discharge their functions;
- to develop scientific and technical studies and research and to work out such operating methods as will make the State capable of counteracting the dangers that threaten its cultural or natural heritage;
- to take the appropriate legal, scientific, technical, administrative and financial measures necessary for identification, protection, conservation, presentation and rehabilitation of this heritage; and
- to foster the establishment or development of national or regional centres for training in the protection, conservation of the cultural and natural heritage and to encourage scientific research in this field.

Once a site has been classified as being of World Heritage standard and is included on the World Heritage List, it is expected that the values and conditions which give it universal significance, and which make it an outstanding example, will be maintained on a permanent basis. This means that actions that would reduce the authenticity or the values of the site, and that would have barred acceptance of the nomination, will not be acceptable after the site is listed. Therefore, the evaluation document upon which the designation of a World Heritage site is based is important as a basic reference; it should identify the values in the site which contribute to its significance in a manner that everyone concerned with it can understand.

2.6   LIST OF WORLD HERITAGE IN DANGER

If the site and its integrity are threatened by serious and specific dangers (ascertained or potential), caused by either man or nature, it may be included (at the request of the State party) on the **List of World Heritage in Danger** with the aim of providing international assistance to the State Party until such time as the threat has terminated (see *Operational Guidelines*, III-A, par. 76-89). Such a threat may be defined as not only external pressure for undesired change in the setting of a site, but also inappropriate proposals for its treatment, eventual use, or both.

2.7   REMOVAL FROM THE WORLD HERITAGE LIST

As described in the *Operational Guidelines* (Section I-E, par. 46-56), a site can be deleted from the World Heritage List in cases where:

- the site has deteriorated to the extent that it has lost those characteristics which determined its inclusion in the World Heritage List; and
- the intrinsic qualities of a world heritage site were already threatened at the time of its nomination by action of man and where the necessary corrective measures, as outlined by the State Party at the time, have not been taken within the time proposed.

2.8   THE EMBLEM

Sites that have been nominated to the World Heritage List may use the World Heritage **Emblem** and the name, symbol or depiction of World Heritage sites. The emblem, designed by Mr Michel Olyff, "symbolizes the interdependence of cultural and natural properties: the central square is a form created by man and the circle represents nature, the two being intimately linked. The emblem is round, like the world, but at the same time it is a symbol of protection." (*Operational Guidelines*, Section VII-A, par. 122-125.)

Chapter 3

EVALUATION FOR CONSERVATION

3.1   SUMMARY

The modern concept of cultural heritage is related to the whole built environment, and should be seen in the ecological context of the world; within this context, the sites on the World Heritage List are distinguished for their outstanding universal value. Conservation policies should be based on a critical process starting with the survey, documentation, and definition of the intrinsic cultural resource, and the values related to it. These values may be divided into two groups: cultural values and contemporary economic values.

The conservation of cultural heritage is a cultural problem. Restoration is not a recipe, but depends on an appropriate understanding of the values contained in the heritage resource. Decisions related to the treatment of World Heritage sites must be based on balanced judgement with due consideration of the objectives of the Convention as a priority. The policy of conservation involves making interventions at various scales and levels of intensity; these are determined by the physical condition, causes of deterioration and anticipated future environment of the cultural resource under treatment. Each case must be considered as a whole, and individually, taking all factors into account. The final aim and the principles of conservation and restoration must be kept in mind; generally the minimum effective intervention has proved to be the best policy.

3.2   WHAT IS CULTURAL HERITAGE TODAY?

The present-day concept of cultural heritage is a result of the process related to the development of contemporary society, its values and its requirements. In the past, attention was given mainly to particular works of art or to major monuments. Massive destruction caused by the world wars and the major industrial development since the 1950s have made people realize that their lives are closely related to the environment in which they live and work. It provides the basis for their cultural identity and a mental and spiritual reference for a balanced quality of life.

❑   *The tendency today is to understand cultural heritage in its broadest sense as containing all the signs that document the activities and achievements of human beings over time.*

Since the Industrial Revolution, the consciousness of the interdependence of man and nature has been steadily weakened. Although natural resources were exploited

– sometimes ruthlessly – in the pre-industrial era, people and the built environment were more dependent upon nature than they are today. In parallel with this, a new problem has been created by the explosive population increase in many countries and the worldwide trend of urbanization: the inconsiderate consumption of non-renewable resources (such as oil and minerals) and the lack of care for resources which are at least partly renewable (such as water, air and forests) have become an international concern.

❑ *Since physical cultural heritage is one of the world's most important non-renewable resources, a special effort is needed to redress the imbalance between our needs and its protection.*

Cultural heritage consists of different types of properties which relate to a variety of settings; they include not only important monuments, historic areas and gardens, but the man-made environment as a whole. Cultural heritage resources may be associated with different values depending on the context, and thus their treatment may differ from case to case.

❑ *The concepts related to the definition of the object, its values and its treatment should be clearly defined in order to avoid confusion in the intent.*

Characterization of cultural heritage, the values related to it and the consequent policy of protection and treatment are referred to in various international documents by UNESCO, notably a series of Recommendations and Conventions. Recommendations provide guidance in the protection of specific types of heritage, such as archaeological sites, historic buildings and historic areas, whereas Conventions, such as the *World Heritage Convention,* are ratified by States Parties as legal instruments.

The most important international policy document is the *International Charter for the Conservation and Restoration of Monuments and Sites,* known as the Venice Charter, which resulted from the Second International Congress of Architects and Technicians of Historic Monuments, held in Venice in 1964. (ICOMOS, founded in 1965, later adopted the Venice Charter as its fundamental doctrinal guideline.)

This document (Appendix A of these *Management Guidelines*) has become a fundamental reference for conservation policies throughout the world.[1]

---

1   For a list of UNESCO Conventions and Recommendations, see Appendix C; the texts are published in: *Conventions and Recommendations of Unesco concerning the protection of the cultural heritage,* UNESCO 1985. Concerning the *Venice Charter,* one may observe that it was written in 1964, during the period of extensive restorations and reconstructions after the damage of the Second World War. The specific problems of that time were emphasized, and less attention given to other concerns that are relevant today. Many attempts have since been made to improve the charter, and in fact numerous international, regional or national recommendations have been written with this purpose; these often refer to specific types of heritage or particular problems. The *Venice Charter,* however, continues to be valid as a proclamation of some of the basic principles.

3.2.1   What defines world cultural heritage ?

In 1972, the concern resulting from increased threats to cultural and natural heritage worldwide, and the desire to provide organized international support for the protection of World Heritage sites and values prompted the General Conference of UNESCO to adopt a special *Convention Concerning the Protection of the World Cultural and Natural Heritage.*

The aim of this Convention is to protect sites that represent "outstanding universal value," as defined the the *Operational Guidelines* (I-C). The World Heritage List, which was established and is maintained on the basis of this Convention, identifies sites in different States Parties that are recognized as resources of international significance, thus meriting special acknowledgement and protection. Together these exemplary resources represent the rich diversity of the world's heritage and, as a consequence, they have important educational connotations.

For the purposes of the Convention, cultural heritage includes monuments, groups of buildings or sites, and these are defined as (Article 1):

  – **monuments**: architectural works, works of monumental sculpture and painting, elements or structures of an archaeological nature, inscriptions, cave dwellings and combinations of features, which are of outstanding universal value from the point of view of history, art or science;

  – **groups of buildings**: groups of separate or connected buildings which, because of their architecture, their homogeneity or their place in the landscape, are of outstanding universal value from the point of view of history, art or science; or

  – **sites**: works of man or the combined works of nature and of man, and areas including archaeological sites which are of outstanding universal value from the historical, aesthetic, ethnological or anthropological points of view.

The basic requirement for the nomination of a site to the World Heritage List is that it represent outstanding universal value. The *Operational Guidelines* define this concept as it is applied to the nomination process, as was addressed in detail in Section 2.3 above.

3.3   WHAT IS PROTECTED IN A MONUMENT OR SITE ?

In the past, restoration theories have often emphasized specific types of treatment, but the conservation and the *mise-en-valeur* of cultural heritage should not be viewed simply as a series of recipes. Today, the concept of cultural heritage is understood in a much broader sense. Consequently, specific protection and conservation strategies are likely to vary considerably according to the context and values associated with each monument or site. Nevertheless, general principles of good conservation practice can serve as a foundation for the identification and protection of heritage resources.

3.3.1   Critical Process

Restoration and conservation should be based on a clear definition of the heritage resource and its relationship to its setting. This definition is part of the critical process aimed at cultivating an appreciation of the heritage as an integral part of present-day society by developing a framework for assessing resource values, establishing management objectives, and preparing presentation and interpretation policies. This process has four distinct steps:

- **Survey**: methodical inspection, survey and documentation of the resource, its historical setting and its physical environment;
- **Definition**: critical-historical definition and assessment of the object and its setting, so giving it its significance;
- **Analysis**: scientific analysis and diagnosis of the material substance and associated structural system with a view towards its conservation; and
- **Strategy**: long-term and short-term programmes for conservation and management of change, including regular inspections, cyclic maintenance and environmental control.

3.3.2   Values related to a heritage resource

Value can be defined as the relative social attribution of qualities to things; values thus depend on society and can change over time. In the case of cultural heritage, particular attention should be paid to what is conceived of as cultural significance, although the economic aspects should not be ignored. Certain values can be related more specifically to the intrinsic aspects of the monument or site – its design, material, and workmanship – while other values can be associated with its location and its relationship to the setting. An historic resource, as a product of the past, has been subjected to degradation caused by natural weathering and functional use. In many cases, the resource has also undergone modifications of various kinds. Such accumulated changes have themselves become part of its historical character and material substance. This material substance is the bearer of the artistic or aesthetic conception of the builders, and of historical testimonies and associated cultural values, both past and present.

❑ *The aim of conservation is to safeguard the quality and values of the resource, protect its material substance and ensure its integrity for future generations.*

3.3.3   Definition of the heritage resource

A heritage resource, an historic monument and at the same time a work of art – whether an historic building, garden, ensemble or site that results from a creative design process – can be defined on the basis of specific concepts. Such a work can generally be conceived as an **artistic whole**, of which its various elements are part. The whole, resulting from a creative process, constitutes a potential unity to which the description and definition of each single part relates.

(A work of art should not be seen as a 'sum total of parts.') One of the aims of the survey and critical-historical assessment is to define the wholeness of the resource and the state of its potential unity.

An historic area, be it a settlement or a cultural landscape, that results from gradual growth or development can be defined in terms of its **historical integrity**. Integrity generally refers to the material completeness and sound condition of an object or site, whereas 'historical integrity' relates to the current form of a heritage resource as a result of growth and changes over time. Identification of such historical integrity can also be relevant in the definition of archaeological sites. The intrinsic qualities of a heritage resource refer to the **quality** of its design, materials, workmanship, setting and relationship to the setting.

Over time, the original heritage resource may be partly damaged, intentionally modified or even destroyed, causing its potential unity to be diminished or lost. On the other hand, an historic resource may, at different periods of its history, become part of a new whole, through which it is redefined as part of a new potential unity; such transformations are part of its historical stratigraphy. Treatments aimed at the restoration of a heritage resource should refer to this new potential unity and should therefore be carried out within the framework defined by it.

Historic areas and their surroundings require particularly careful study and consideration since individual monuments and historic buildings are only part of the larger ensemble of the heritage resource. The UNESCO *Recommendation concerning Safeguarding and Contemporary Role of Historic Areas*, formulated in Nairobi in 1976, provides the following guideline (General Principles, II,2):

> Every historic area and its surroundings should be considered in their totality as a coherent whole whose balance and specific nature depend on the fusion of the parts of which it is composed and which include human activities as much as the buildings, the spatial organization and the surroundings. All valid elements, including human activities, however modest, thus have a significance in relation to the whole which must not be disregarded.

The whole of historic areas should thus not be considered only in relation to an architectural framework; it should also include the human values related to its social and economic context. Of particular importance is also the question of historic parks and landscapes. Throughout history, in many countries, garden design has been very closely associated with architecture (e.g., China, England, France, India, Iran, Italy and Japan). It is important that, in defining the site, due attention be given to these features, requiring proper archaeological research, and knowledge of the history and principles of garden design, in order not to lose these important and often fragile features in a rehabilitation process. In recent years, much international attention has been given to historic parks and gardens, and their documentation; guidelines have been developed for their proper maintenance, conservation and restoration.[2]

Particularly since the 1980s, with the increased awareness of the importance of the relationship and interdependence of the built and the natural environment, the issue of protecting cultural landscapes has become significant in many countries, both in industrialized areas and in areas undergoing rapid development (where modern development often ignores the values of the existing ecological or traditional cultural context and the need to maintain existing resources). The question of defining criteria for the nomination of cultural landscapes to the World Heritage List has been under study, but whether or not these are implemented, there remains the urgent necessity to take due care not only of specific monuments or groups of buildings, **but also to provide sufficient planning tools for the control and balanced development of their wider context.**

3.3.4   Historical time line[3]

The relationship of a heritage resource, such as a work of art, an historic building or an historic town to time and history may be broken down into in three phases:

- the first phase, which resulted in the **creation** of the object;
- the second phase, which extends from the end of the creation phase to the present time; and
- the third phase, which is associated with the perception of the monument in our consciousness at the **present time**.

This sequence of phases forms the **historical time line** of the resource. This historical time line is irreversible. It is a product of the specific cultural, social, economic and political conditions of the phases that contributed to the creation and development of the heritage resource. This linkage with specific historical phases becomes a fundamental reference for the evaluation of an historic resource. Alois Riegl, an Austrian art historian and conservator, developed the concept of *Kunstwollen*[4] in 1903 to express the fact that an object created at a given time both reflects the artistic trends of its period and contributes to these trends. A heritage resource that is substantially reconstructed today would become a product of the present.

❑ *Since a heritage resource is* **unique** *in relation to historical time, it is* **non-renewable**.

3.3.5   What is authenticity?

Authenticity is a crucial aspect in the assessment of heritage resources. Generally speaking, authenticity is ascribed to a heritage resource that is

---

2   The ICOMOS International Committee for Historic Gardens can be consulted for a network of experts in the conservation of historic gardens.

3   This corresponds to the *tempo storico* in Brandi's writings.

4   See Riegl, 1903, and also Holly, 1984, in the bibliography.

materially *original* or *genuine* as it was constructed and as it has aged and weathered in time.[5] With regard to an historic monument or site conceived as a work of art, being 'authentic' can be understood in relation to the creative process that produced it as a genuine product of its time, and includes the effects of its passage through historic time. (Being 'authentic' should not be confused with 'identical'; e.g., modern reconstruction can be identical with the historic form, but is not authentic.) The 1994 *Nara Document on Authenticity* stresses the credibility or truthfulness of the information sources for the assessment of authenticity, and notes that the diversity of cultures and heritage can be understood as an irreplaceable source of spiritual and intellectual richness for all humankind.

Authenticity derives from the definition of the resource, and so authenticity may be understood in different ways depending on the context of its historical significance.

❑   *In the case of a heritage resource, its historical authenticity should generally reflect the significant phases of construction and utilization in different phases of its* **historical time line.**

Authenticity can be jeopardized by the destruction of historical strata, the modern replacement of original elements (particularly if based on conjecture) and the addition of new elements. A heritage resource that has passed the **test of authenticity** maintains its original integrity, as created or as it has evolved through its historical time line. While various aspects of the heritage resource should be analysed in order to define the degree of authenticity, it is important to arrive at a comprehensive judgement – i.e., a single aspect is not sufficient. According to the *Operational Guidelines,* four aspects of authenticity should be considered:

- –   authenticity in design,
- –   authenticity in materials,
- –   authenticity in workmanship, or
- –   authenticity in setting.

To be nominated to the World Heritage List, the heritage resource must maintain its integrity with respect to these four types of authenticity. If, for example, the original resource is destroyed, a copy would not meet the criteria since the material authenticity would be lost. Authenticity in materials is a primary criterion for authenticity in design and in workmanship, which, together with authenticity in setting, define the cultural heritage resource. On the other hand, at the same time, most historic resources are altered by the actions of nature and utilization; these changes are part of the **historical stratification** of the resource.

In addition, the concept of *Authenticity in the socio-cultural context* is one that urgently requires consideration.

---

5   The word *authentic* may be understood as *original, first hand* (as opposed to *copy*), or as *real, actual, genuine* (as opposed to *pretended*). *Shorter Oxford English Dictionary.*

3.4   WHAT VALUES INFLUENCE TREATMENTS?

Many values may be associated with heritage resources; those that are deemed significant will provide justification for its protection and conservation. Such values range from historical to commercial, and a single resource may possess conflicting values that make management decisions especially difficult; moreover, value judgements may change over time.[6]

When dealing with World Heritage sites, considerations should include both
- cultural values, and
- contemporary socio-economic values.

The presence or absence of these values will lead to the safeguarding and preservation of cultural heritage resources or, in other instances, could lead to their neglect and destruction. For example, nationalistic or political values could provide a motivation for the protection and restoration of a resource, but these same values could cause the loss of resource that does not meet the prevailing political conception of significance.

3.4.1   Cultural values

Cultural values that are associated with heritage resources and their relationship to present-day observers are necessarily subjective (i.e., they depend on interpretations that reflect our time). These assessments will determine the degree of general interest in the object and in its setting, the interpretation of its intrinsic cultural character and the development of treatment policies. The recognition of **outstanding universal significance** in World Heritage sites and their resultant treatment should be defined on the basis of these assessments with respect to historical substance and archaeological potential.

The aim of the groupings given below is to help identify the various types of values that are often discussed, and to understand their relationship to the cultural resource, the site and its context. The question of appropriate treatment is further discussed in Chapter 8, *Treatments and Authenticity*.

Cultural values can be classified in a number of ways.

Identity value (based on recognition):

Values: This group of values is related to the emotional ties of society to specific objects or sites. It can include the following features: age, tradition, continuity, memorial, legendary; wonder, sentiment, spiritual, religious; and symbolic, political, patriotic and nationalistic.

---

6   Riegl, writing in 1903, was already analysing in detail the different values related to historic monuments at the beginning of the 20th century. (See bibliography)

Impact: Consisting often of emotional perceptions, this group of values has a strong impact on the safeguarding, conservation and restoration of the resource. While these values could strengthen the treatment of the resource, they could also cause over-restoration. At the same time, the lack of this identity could lead to neglect and destruction. These values can be promoted through education and training.

Relative artistic or technical value (based on research):

Values: This group of values is based on scientific and critical historical evaluations and assessments of the importance of the design of the heritage resource, and the significance of its technical, structural and functional concept and workmanship.

Impact: These values result from research carried out by professionals, with the intention of demonstrating the relative significance of the resource in relation to its own time, to other periods, and to the present. They provide a basis for classification and listing, as well as strategy for treatment.

Rarity value (based on statistics):

Values: This group of values relates the resource to other constructions of the same type, style, builder, period, region or some combination of these; they define the resource's rarity, representativeness or uniqueness.

Impact: This group of values is related to the two previous value groups, and influences the level of protection accorded to the resource. A high rarity value may reinforce the significance of the qualities that have outstanding universal value, and therefore strengthen the possibility of listing as a World Heritage site.

3.4.2 Contemporary socio-economic values

Use values are related to present-day society and its socio-economic and political infrastructures. The following categories have been identified:

Economic value:

Values: Since economics encourages the best allocation of resources to fit a wide range of needs, the economic value may not be restricted to a financial value. In terms of cultural heritage, economic value may be understood as a value generated by the heritage resource or by conservation action.

Impact: Economic values have four potential sources of revenue: tourism, commerce, use and amenities. The mismanagement of any one of these sources could lead to the undesirable development, or even the destruction, of the heritage resource; this is often the case when profit value is erroneously measured instead of using a more appropriate collective cost-benefit approach.

Functional value:

Values: Functional value is related to economic value, as it involves the continuity of the original type of function or the initiation of a compatible use
of a building or an area. In a ruined structure, the original functional value
is lost, but a new one has been found in serving programmatic requirements for resource interpretation, or as a venue for activities such as the
visual and performing arts.

Impact: Continuity of traditional functions reinforces the meaning of sites in a
manner that can never be accomplished by interpretative exhibits. An
appropriate use will favour conservation; an inappropriate or ill-conceived adaptive use may cause degradation, undesirable changes or
demolition.

Educational value:

Values: The educational value of a heritage resource includes its potential for
cultural tourism, and the awareness of culture and history that it promotes
as a means of integrating historic resources in present-day life.

Impact: The appropriate integration of World Heritage sites into educational
programmes is essential. Emphasis on tourism, however, could lead to
unjustified reconstructions or the destruction of original fabric, causing
a loss of non-renewable archaeological evidence.

Social value:

Values: The social value of a heritage resource is related to traditional social
activities and to compatible present-day use. It involves contemporary
social interaction in the community, and plays a role in establishing
social and cultural identity.

Impact: Social values can generate the concern for the local environment that
leads to maintenance and repair of the fabric of a heritage resource; a
lack of this social coherence and appreciation can handicap conservation.
Such grass-roots interest has been the driving force behind the Civic
Amenity movements.

Political value:

Values: Political value is often related to specific events in the history of the
heritage resource with respect to its region or country. The present-day
significance of the resource could be influenced by these events insofar
as they coincide with the intentions of contemporary political priorities.

Impact: The political significance of a monument or site may assist in raising
funds and drawing the attention of the general public to safeguarding and
protection. On the other hand, ill-advised action may lead to undesired
development and destruction of authenticity.

The above grouping of values should be considered as indicative, and may be compared with the values recognized in national or local assessments of heritage resources; they can also provide a useful framework and reference for a more detailed evaluation process.

Many of these values – particularly contemporary socio-economic values – can have both positive and negative impacts on the cultural resource, depending on the type of value and on the emphasis that is given to it in the overall assessment. It is therefore vital to make a clear statement of the values for which a particular cultural heritage resource has been nominated to the World Heritage List. These specific values and the question of the authenticity of the site are referred to in the evaluation document prepared by ICOMOS for the World Heritage Committee at the time of nomination. This document should always be available as a reference for the conservation managers of the site.

If the values for which the site has been nominated, particularly its 'outstanding universal value,' are diminished or threatened, the site may be recommended for inscription to the List of World Heritage in Danger. This will also necessitate a request for technical assistance from the World Heritage Committee in order to support the efforts of the local authority in the management of necessary interventions.

4.1   INTRODUCTION

❑ *Planning, programming and budgeting is a continuing process that must be reviewed and updated at regular intervals.*

The planning process should be a multidisciplinary activity with input from experts in matters relating to the significance of the site. This means that the values in the site should be listed and, if possible, put in order of priority.

The inevitable contradictions of the planning process should be resolved first by examining the implications of all viable alternatives, and then deciding which is least harmful to the significance of the heritage site. Open discussion among experts can lead to creative solutions that may enhance the significance or messages of the site, but this process takes time.

❑ *Reviews at regular intervals can, if the planning process is scientific and logical, correct mistakes and refine concepts.*

The assumptions upon which a plan is based should be clearly stated. With time, it is possible that the original assumptions will change. Some assumptions are culturally inspired, others may be based on fashionable or political trends. All assumptions should be analysed. The long-term management plan (up to 30 years) should integrate all the information contained in documentation and action plans. There also should be medium-term plans (for, say, 5 years) and annual project plans.

4.2   MANAGEMENT

4.2.1   Objectives of Management

The State Party may wish to achieve the objectives of coordinated and integrated planning and management of the World Heritage site by different means, and could therefore consider the following points:

- If the State Party has more than one World Heritage site, should the sites be managed individually or collectively?
- If managed collectively, will the individual sites receive proper attention?
- Historic towns or villages that are included on the World Heritage List will probably be managed individually, but should be understood in relation to their territory, and may need enlarged buffer areas.

- If the State Party has a national council for conservation of heritage, should it be given the task of managing the World Heritage sites? If so, should creation of management units be considered?

There are many ways in which the historical, artistic, technical and craft skills of academics, professionals and artisans can be mobilized effectively, with delegated responsibility and accountability, so that the cultural resources of the site are protected and handed over intact to the next generation. These *Management Guidelines* aim at helping such a Commission to execute its complex tasks in conserving all World Heritage sites.

4.2.2   Data on which the management plan is based

The General Management Plan should take into account national and local plans as far as they apply, as well as forecasts of demographic growth or decline, economic factors, motor traffic projections and industrial zoning. This plan should also be based on inspections and reports by suitable multidisciplinary teams.

One of the principal actions to be taken is to guarantee that the resource is systematically recorded and documented before, during and after any intervention. Once the intervention has taken place, what was removed or altered is lost for ever if not properly documented. **Recording and documentation is an ongoing activity throughout a conservation process.**

In general, the historical use of the site should be maintained, as this is the reason for its significance. Nothing stays still, however, and change is inevitable. The art of planning is to guide change in a way that will, if possible, enhance the significance of the site by minimum intervention at key points. This invokes two questions:

- How to find the key points? and
- What is the minimum intervention?

These questions are for the planning team to consider. In addition, other aspects should be considered for the general management plan, including:

- investigation of plans for alternative use and their application, together with assessment of their feasibility and cost;
- designation of use zones, if necessary;
- in historic towns or areas, control of the height, size and scale of new, infill building;
- designation of conservation areas, with subsidies to encourage both maintenance and suitable improvements, especially to the streetscape;
- control of electrical cables and other wires, and of signs, shop fronts and advertisements; and

- establishment of zones for compatible activities of benefit to all users of heritage sites, excluding – by preventing permission for – incompatible uses.

4.2.3   Inventory and documentation

❑ *A full inventory and documentation of the buildings with their contents and the landscape of the site should be prepared.*

This inventory should provide a brief description of the resource, the important dates in its history, and its location. Such skeleton information can be fleshed out with references. Since there are many different methods of making an inventory, the one that harmonizes most easily with the State Party's existing procedures should be adopted.[1]

Proper inventory and documentation are an invaluable tool in the event of disasters such as fire, flood or theft; for safety reasons, at least two copies of this documentation should be kept in separate places (one in fireproof storage). For insurance purposes, movable objects in the inventory should be classified as one of the following:

- irreplaceable,
- replaceable, or
- reproducible.

The inventory can also be catalogued using a computerized system. Development of modern technology has made it possible to acquire the hardware and software at a fraction of previous costs; one can now say that the computer has become a necessary tool for the sophisticated management of World Heritage sites, and that it can be made available to developing countries. A computerized system will demand quicker and more positive response from the site staff.

The new generation of personal computers makes it possible for each major site to have its own computer. A competent consultant with experience of setting up computers for the documentation of cultural heritage should be employed to help prepare a purpose-made thesaurus and train staff in preparation of material.

It should be stressed that a computer is only as good as the data supplied to it, but – given good field work – it is an invaluable tool for management since it can process basic data in so many different ways. It also implies that all staff concerned are using the same information, which can be updated, revised or expanded by a single operation.

However, one point that must be stressed is that of compatibility – i.e., that the form in which the data is stored should conform to accepted international standards

---

1   The 1996 ICOMOS Recording and Documentation Principles, included as Appendix F, provide some useful concepts on this topic.

so that the data can be easily shared, or easily transferred to successor systems. In this context, the need for simple operating manuals for users – in their own language – and the establishment of minimum data requirements should be made clear.

Looking ahead, data currently being collected should be stored in its most dis-aggregated form to allow maximum flexibility in its future use.

For sites that cover a large area or have complex urban elements, consideration could be given to the possibility of using geographical information system (GIS) techniques to efficiently manage the data.

❑ *It is important to remember, however, that priority must be given to conserving endangered buildings rather than purchasing equipment.*

The question of the management of the recording, documentation and information of cultural resources is a key issue in the conservation process. Before starting it is necessary to prepare a work plan, which clearly defines the resource and its context, the objectives and the extent of documentation, the recommended levels of documentation, the technologies available or that will have to be acquired, the time frame, as well as requirements for the organization and execution of the project.

❑ *Heritage resources should be systematically recorded using photographs and other suitable methods.*

Satellite photos, aerial photography, as well as aerial and terrestrial photogrammetry, are invaluable aids to forming a quantitative inventory of both natural and man-made sites. However, the technology to be used in the recording process depends both on the type and character of the resource as well as on the objectives and the utilization of the records. Several types of techniques may be considered either independently or in combination depending on the case; at one extreme, this could include hand recording, record photography, rectified photography or video; at the other extreme, the use of electronic theodolites or stereo-photogrammetry, with computer-aided design (CAD) or image processing. The recommended levels of recording could include an initial photographic recording, a preliminary, and a detailed record, which could be partial (for operational needs) or complete (for future reference).

4.2.4   Information management

Considering the amount of information required and produced for each site, a clear **heritage information-management policy** is required. This is necessary also for the purposes of standardizing procedures, ensuring that the information is in a form that is compatible with that from other sources, and thus exchangeable – both in the national context, and at a regional or international level. Even greater emphasis should be given to this aspect in connection with World Heritage sites.

❑ *Most heritage databases have so far been developed in isolation, often without consultation or links outside the immediate group, thus multiplying the efforts. It will therefore be necessary to start a process of unification of standards, in order to facilitate accessibility and interpretation of records, to facilitate the process of preparation of records and make it easier to provide a comprehensive coverage without forgetting essential issues in the process.*

The published literature relating to the heritage site may take a long time to collect and it may be necessary to arrange for photographic or microform copies to be made of documents held elsewhere. Ideally, these should be **catalogued**, preferably using the UNISIST system, and skillfully **abstracted** so as to enhance the availability of essential information through the computerized inventory. Documents dealing with policy and research should be stored, together with copies of all resolutions and minutes of meetings leading up to the establishment of the site as World Heritage status.

While access to these documents by researchers, students and interested members of the public should be encouraged, the proper management of the documents in perpetuity must be given primary consideration. Trained librarians and archivists, adequate space and proper storage conditions are essential. All items should be examined by a trained conservator and treated if necessary before being stored.

❑ *Fire protection for documentation should be given priority and, if any type of natural disaster is a hazard, the risk should be assessed and suitable precautions taken, such as safe, off-site storage of duplicate copies.*

❑ *Management should establish* **a regular annual review** *of the situation and receive a report from the person responsible for document preservation; this person could also be identified as the* **disaster response officer** *together with an alternate.*

To prepare a well-documented **maintenance plan,** the work of experts such as engineers and art historians has to be coordinated and evaluated by an architect generalist, who should view the problems in the context of the whole; this generalist should have enough scientific, technical, artistic and historical or cultural knowledge to appreciate the contribution of the specialist experts. Experts should **communicate** their ideas and opinions in clear, jargon-free language.

4.2.5   Research planning

- What issues demand research?
- How should research be managed?

These simple questions do not have simple answers. Every World Heritage site contains a wide range of elements deserving of research, much of which is purely academic. Close **liaison should be maintained with universities** and other facilities interested in the cultural resources, and the collection of all pertinent documentation related to the site is obviously essential.

Nowadays, universities encourage thesis subjects that stimulate creative and original research. Students who contribute to the knowledge of cultural resources through their research may become valuable staff members of the site commission in the future.

To provide answers to the two simple questions asked at the start of this section, it is advisable to set up a **research coordination committee** for the site. This committee, answering to the Site Commission, could organize **long-term programmes** involving a succession of researchers or **short-term programmes** for individuals; it could also set the goals, establish the work plans and schedules and review the progress of all research projects, as well as advise on the award of related grants and contracts.

4.2.6   General schedule

The production, selection and approval of the general management plan implies the completion of the following preparatory steps:

✓ The **significance** of the site is documented and appreciated.

✓ The **objective** of the plan is clearly defined.

✓ The **evidence** and opinions of appropriate experts has been considered. Inspections and reports have been made.

✓ Alternative courses of **action** and their effects have been studied and documented.

We are now ready to select the least bad management plan and submit it for approval.

✓ The plan should start with a **statement of the management aim;** this should be expressed in terms that all staff can appreciate.

✓ The **minimum appropriate level of maintenance** should be defined that is compatible with respecting the significance of the cultural resource, the needs of users, and the local climatic constraints.

✓ An outline of the State Party's **planning regulations,** as they affect the whole site, should be prepared.

✓ Other **plans and legislation** that affect the site should be considered by the Site Commission and integrated into the overall schemes of management, maintenance, development or research.

✓ The general management plan should identify **personnel** required to operate and maintain the site, and define their tasks, *inter alia* with respect to
different scenarios, long- or short-term activities, and budget implications.

✓ Proposals for the **development** of facilities should be included in the
management plan, but under a separate budget heading.

Projects can be brought forward for approval by stages:

✓ Approval of the concept.

✓ Feasibility studies and approximate costs of alternatives.

✓ Design studies and approval of selected schemes – the prescription.

✓ Detailed design and costing.

✓ Fiscal approval and programming.

✓ Start and execution.

✓ Documentation of project.

❑ *Research and study should be planned and programmed.*

In general, it is advisable to award contracts to independent experts or academic
institutions with an interest in the study of the resource. Model contract forms
should be prepared, with standard clauses dealing with details, copyright,
publication and storage, in order to ensure consistency across activities.

❑ *All researchers should submit annual progress reports.*

The annual progress report should have two parts: a technical one covering in detail
all work done, results, costs, implications of findings, etc., and a popular one
suitable for public information purposes, highlighting activities and significant
findings. Such reports serve as valuable tools. The popular version is good for
public relations and fund raising, while the technical one forms part of the ongoing
documentation archive of the site.

4.2.7 Administration

❑ *The role of the administration and management team is to conserve the
heritage resource and to serve the public interest, provided this is not
detrimental to the site.*

Responsibilities should be decentralized and individual staff members should be
allowed to make their own immediate decisions within the context of the
management plan and their pre-defined responsibilities; this should lead to
increased efficiency and job satisfaction.

Job satisfaction will attract and retain good staff, which is the best guarantee of good work.

❑ *To achieve effective management, all staff should be aware of the guidelines controlling the work of the whole administration.*

Administrative tasks are simplified when the entire property is managed by a single landlord. In some circumstances, ownership of all the properties could be the long-term objective of the Site Commission. Although this would make management simpler, there may be social costs implicit in changing ownership, such as the possible disruption of community life and use patterns; the alternative of strong town planning controls and public education could be more beneficial.

4.2.8 Cost control and policy

Controlling the costs of conservation projects is critical. Much time and money is wasted, and damage caused to cultural buildings, due to lack of clear concepts of conservation policy, and firm control in execution.

❑ *Control must be delegated to one competent person after the policy has been decided by a multidisciplinary group of experienced experts.*

Conservation policy for an individual building should be based on a thorough inspection and any other required studies. The policy should never be determined by a single individual, as the responsibility is too great, but it is possible for one person, like the conductor of an orchestra, to be in charge of implementation.

4.2.9 Legal instruments

Legal instruments and regulations that respect the social and employment regulations of the State Party should be drafted, including:

- an **Act** to establish the site as World Cultural Heritage and set up a Site Commission;
- **statutes** for the **Site Commission** and **rules governing financial procedures**. As the Commission should be at arm's length from the government of the State Party, its funding should ideally be in five-year grants (adjusted for inflation); this will enable it to do its forward planning in confidence and minimize ill-considered interference;
- **staff regulations** and **conditions of employment**; and
- **empowerment of the Site Commission** to undertake and award contracts for activities within its sphere of competence.

4.2.10   Programming

Programming is related to the available staff and budget. Resource problems will have to be identified in advance and assigned priorities in accordance with their urgency:

- **Immediate** problems create a potential danger to the public or risk to the resource, and should be dealt with first. The fiscal plan should allocate a contingency reserve for dealing with immediate problems as soon as possible after they are reported by the responsible person. Of course, natural disasters might be too big to be dealt with in this way, but typical immediate items include repairing damage to buildings after strong winds or clearing paths in a park site.

- **Urgent** problems, if not dealt with promptly, will cause further damage or decay and should be addressed next. In buildings, outbreaks of fungal or termite attack should be dealt with urgently, and rainwater disposal systems should be kept in good working order to prevent decay.

- **Necessary** problems constitute the bulk of the work necessary to preserve the resource over the five-year (or other) funding period.

- **Desirable** items may be considered as part of the **Development Budget**.

- **Keep Watch** items should be kept under observation and studied to see whether they are serious or not. These include foundation movements in a building, or the performance of installations.

- **Future liabilities**, such as replacement of obsolescent plant, the renewal of roofs or the replanting of a garden, should also be reviewed.

The interaction and efficient programming of all foreseeable factors should be considered by the Site Commission acting on proposals submitted by the Director. Projects can then be defined and specified for execution.

4.3   PROGRAMME REVIEW AND FUTURE PLANNING

The State Party possesses an internal network for communication and the flow of documentation within the responsible ministry, headquarters staff of the Site Commission, regional and local planning offices and the site staff. It is desirable to develop an interface between State Party professionals, site staff and an international consultancy body. As has already been suggested, senior professionals of the State Party might be incorporated into the Site Commission. It is important that this body come under one ministry with an assigned mandate to deal directly with the World Heritage Convention, and that other relevant ministries be kept informed.

The World Heritage Committee understands systematic monitoring and reporting as the continuous process of observing the conditions of a World Heritage site with periodic reporting on its state of conservation. While on-site monitoring is the prime responsibility of the State Party, there is a need for a constant two-way communication between those responsible for the site and the World Heritage Committee; this should include reports on:

- status and current condition,
- planning and action documents,
- requests for funds and technical assistance, and
- reports of threats, either current or expected.

4.4   BUDGETING

The formulation of a budget entails knowledge and experience of similar operations. Local conditions and salary scales vary greatly, but, in general, conservation of cultural heritage is labour intensive and demands special knowledge and dedication. For the first five years after the establishment of the Site Commission it will be difficult to formulate the budget accurately, so generous provision by the State Party will be necessary to establish the Commission and initiate its activities. For efficient execution of its programme, the Site Commission must be able to plan five years ahead in confidence, and to retain any surplus funds that may accrue from one year to the next, since development and research projects tend to run more slowly than planned. This fiscal provision is essential in order for the skilled labour available to be kept in full employment.

4.4.1   Annual budget

Annual budgeting should be established within a longer-term financial plan. The budget will be divided into several parts, with sub-headings according to tasks. To manage such a complex operation and monitor the implementation of the budget by quarterly or monthly and even spot checks, an efficient system of accounting is essential. It pays to introduce modern accounting equipment and qualified personnel. The accountant should report to the Director. Annual accounts should be audited by independent accountants who will report, through the Director, to the Site Commission. Heads of departments will manage such funds as are delegated to them by the Director, and will be accountable for their correct use. If any budget item is likely to be exceeded the Director's sanction must be obtained **before** expenditure is incurred or committed. It should be remembered that planning, programming and budgeting is a continual process that must be reviewed and updated at regular, pre-determined intervals.

4.4.2   UNESCO's role

UNESCO's World Heritage Centre acts as the secretariat to the World Heritage Committee, which can provide, from the World Heritage Fund, financial assistance to States Parties for various purposes. This can include assistance in training, in technical missions and equipment. The procedure for the application has been determined by the World Heritage Committee and publicized accordingly. Funds are provided by the World Heritage Committee for technical assistance or treatment only if management plans have been approved, and a professional report on the condition of the site is submitted at regular intervals according to the instructions of the World Heritage Committee.

The international bodies recognized by the World Heritage Convention are:

- The International Centre for the Study of the Preservation and Restoration of Cultural Property (ICCROM);
- The International Council on Monuments and Sites (ICOMOS) for cultural heritage sites, and
- The International Union for the Conservation of Nature and Natural Resources (IUCN) for natural heritage sites.

In collaboration with the UNESCO World Heritage Centre, these bodies will collaborate with the States Parties on issues related to the management of their sites. Having accepted the *Operational Guidelines*, the World Heritage Committee intends to re-evaluate and update them every five years in order to keep abreast of current management and operational requirements.

An important issue in relation to the management of World Heritage Sites is to establish a process that gives a solid basis for international collaboration between those responsible for the site management and the various international bodies, such as the World Heritage Committee, UNESCO, ICCROM and ICOMOS. This process may include cycles of technical meetings to discuss management issues, systems of reporting on progress, and also participation in training activities either within the context of the site itself or in regional or international courses and seminars, such as those organized by ICCROM in Rome.

4.5   CHECKLIST FOR MANAGEMENT

✓ Do you have a management plan for the maintenance strategy of your World Heritage site, and is this plan regularly updated?

✓ Have long-, medium- and short-term objectives been clearly defined?

✓ Have the values, priorities and the least harmful action been taken into consideration in this plan?

✓ Is there an inventory, and has the resource been adequately recorded and documented?

✓ Is the relevant documentation concerning the site accessible?

✓ Has the site documentation been duplicated in a safe place?

✓ Is there a fire protection plan, and is it practised on a regular basis?

✓ Do you have the disaster hazard plan for your region?

✓ Have a disaster response officer and alternate been designated?

✓ Have contacts for effective research programmes been established with universities and other institutions?

✓ Do the laws and regulations that are being applied reflect the latest technical knowledge and attitudes to conservation?

✓ Is their application effective? If not, where do they fail?

✓ Is the management infrastructure adequate and effective in fulfilling its role?

✓ Have lines of communication been established with international organizations concerned with preservation of World Heritage?

Chapter 5

MANAGEMENT BY RESOURCE PROJECTS

5.1   MANAGEMENT PLAN PREPARATION

The preparation of a management plan for a World Heritage site implies the consideration of **all** its resources. A resource constitutes an identifiable part of a World Heritage site. Some sites may possess only one resource, such as primitive rock carvings, whereas others may have several; the resources of a large building include its fabric, carving, glass, furnishings, textiles, etc.

5.1.1   Procedure

The following steps are involved in preparing a management plan:

- initial survey of the site
- site description and boundary definition
- identification of resources
- evaluation of resources
- formulation of objectives and consideration of constraints
- definition of projects
- work programme and annual plans
- execution of works
- recording, reporting and review of results
- storage of information and data
- revision of site description and re-evaluation
- formulation of revised objectives and reconsideration of constraints
- definition of further projects
- revised work programme and next annual plan

5.1.2   Requirements

The first requirement of site management is the conservation and protection of its cultural resources and, where possible, the enhancement of features of special interest. Once this requirement is fulfilled, the site can be used for a number of other purposes such as education, research, tourism and even occupation; it goes without saying, however, that the integrity of a World Heritage site must be maintained.

Detailed management plans for resources need not be complicated or lengthy. Provided the main objectives are known and the site staff is properly qualified, resources can be managed on the basis of care and maintenance. There should be a full review every 3-5 years, but the system should be able to accommodate adjustments which allow results of site works or unexpected developments to be fed back and integrated into a rolling management programme.

5.1.3 Preparation and consultation procedures

The procedures followed during the preparation of a management plan, which are distinct from the format of the plan itself, imply a team effort. Even the simplest management plan involves enough complexity, in its preparation or execution, to justify the involvement of several skills, such as architects, archaeologists, historians, engineers and town planners. A multidisciplinary team approach has the potential advantage of producing a clear rationale of objectives and avoiding the difficulties that can arise when only a single individual is responsible for the management of a resource. This is particularly important in order to establish a continuity of objectives over a period that will usually outlast any individual member of staff. Whatever the make-up of the team, most of the initiative for preparing the management plan will lie with one or two people, usually the architect or archaeologist and administrator.

Preparation of the management plan will also involve consultation outside the team and consideration of management plan objectives for similar resources. Sources of information include:

- **Research- and information-orientated sources**, including local and national archives, universities, town planning reports and voluntary special interest groups; and
- **Management-orientated sources**, including property owners, tenants, neighbours and other land managers.

Consultation with owners, tenants and neighbours involves discussion of any potential threats identified when the site was proposed as a World Heritage site.

When a draft of the management plan is completed, it should be scrutinized by a central government group at national level. Such scrutiny allows more detailed examination, debate about objectives in relation to other sites, and an assessment of the financial implications of the work programme. A complete set of approved management plans, as well as the annual progress reports relating to them, should be kept by the national government, and it may be practical for regions to maintain a collection of these documents as well.

Because of the complexity of the preparation process, the range of consultations involved and the conflicting demands on staff time, the preparation of a resource management plan is likely to take from three months (in the case of the simplest sites) to two years (in the more complex large sites and cities). As previously mentioned, however, it is possible to proceed with the management of the site on the basis of a partial plan.

5.2   REPORTING

5.2.1   Short-term reporting and review

The efficiency of management depends on reporting at regular intervals, whether monthly, quarterly or annually. The management plan will outline for site staff the annual programme of projects and their associated costs, time allocations, etc. There would be two types of reports on these projects:

- monthly or quarterly assessments of the progress of each individual project, which will allow priorities and time allocations to be modified, if necessary, as early as possible; and
- an annual summary of the progress of individual projects (or groups of projects), together with associated financial and staff-time costs.

The content of the reports should cover all the projects within the annual work plan. It may be useful to classify the projects according to their scope, type of work and duration.

Since **Annual Work Plans** could be subject to slippage and delay, an annual summary of their progress – the **Annual Progress Report** (which should be project-based) – is necessary. This report summarizes the information provided in the monthly or quarterly reports and allows comparisons to be made with the list of projects proposed in the overall management plan. It also enables shortfalls and problems to be identified and modifications in subsequent work plans to be made.

5.2.2   Long-term reporting and review

Management plans should be based on a minimum period of five years, at the end of which a review is necessary. At that time, the Annual Progress Reports for the preceding management plan should be summarized for incorporation in the new one. This allows information on the progress of previous plans to be transmitted and provides a way of dealing with continuity, changes in personnel and the accumulation of increased knowledge about the site.

5.2.3   Format of the management plan

A standard format is essential to the successful operation of a uniform planning system, providing a framework for consistent interpretation and easy cross-referencing of information relating to a wide range of resources. The standardization of management activities associated with individual sites is also crucial to planning the management and monitoring the progress of World Heritage sites as a group. A further advantage of a standard format is the relative ease with which statistical and other information can be extracted as required for particular purposes. The format recommended here has three distinct parts: (1) a description of the site; (2) evaluation and objectives; (3) prescription, together with a mandatory preface summarizing the status and context of the site. More specifically, as a working basis, the format below is recommended.

ANNUAL MANAGEMENT PLAN
for {resource name, or project designation}
of {Site name} for {period}

Preface
  —   Status and context of site

Part 1:   Description of the Site

1.1   General information
  —   Location, summary description, tenure
  —   Maps, charts, photographs

1.2   Cultural information
  —   Anthropological, ethnographic, archaeological, historical, art historical, architectural, technological, scientific

1.3   Environmental information
  —   Climate, hydrology, geology, geomorphology, seismology, soils, man-made hazards

1.4   Interests
  —   Land use and resource use history
  —   Public and private interests, ownership pattern
  —   Economic interests, including tourism

1.5   Appendices to Part 1
  —   List of references for Part 1
  —   List of amendments to Part 1

Part 2:   Evaluation and Objectives

2.1   Conservation status of the site
  —   World Heritage Site status, historic status
  —   Indication of potentially damaging operations or threats
  —   Resource definition and boundary

2.2   Evaluation of site features and potential
- Cultural values related to the original historical material and the archaeological potential of the site (authenticity of materials, workmanship, design and setting)
- Cultural values associated with the site (universal significance, memorial, legendary and sentimental values, relative art value, uniqueness)
- Contemporary economic values and use values

2.3   Identification and confirmation of important features
- Ideal management objectives
- Factors influencing management
- Operational objectives and management options
- Conservation management options
- Use management options
- Study and research options
- Education and interpretation options

2.4   Appendices to Part 2
- List of references for Part 2
- List of amendments to Part 2

Part 3:   Prescription for Overall Site Management

3.1   Projects
- Project identification, title, classification
- Project register
- Project descriptions

3.2   Work schedule
- Annual work plan
- Relationship of the annual plan to the medium- and long-term plans

3.3   Costs and staging of works

3.4   Appendices to Part 3
- References to Part 3
- List of amendments to Part 3

Bibliography
- Selected bibliography and register of unpublished material
- General bibliography
- Amendments to bibliography

5.2.4   Comments on the format

This recommended format represents the logical sequence in which the Site Management Plan should, ideally, be written. To meet immediate management requirements, however, Part 3 – Prescription for overall site management – may be written first, but this should not be attempted before completing an initial appraisal of the site's important features and operational objectives. As well as outlining the total work required, Part 3 can be used to guide a continuing programme of work.

The management plan should be presented in terms of a working document, rather than a bound publication: the use of a loose-leaf format in a binder will allow drafts and revisions to be incorporated into any or several sections simultaneously. If a section cannot be completed (e.g., where no information is available for Section 1.3 on Environmental information), or if no assessment of the site's potential has been made, a brief statement, with a date, should be provided. Subsequent re-appraisals or completed sections can be inserted at a later date. Where sections or statements in previous management plans are still considered to be appropriate, they may be included in the relevant section, with appropriate references and notes.

5.2.5   Presentation of management plans

The following methods of presentation are recommended:

- Use a loose-leaf format in a suitable binder.
- Use the contents referencing system given above. Where a section or sub-section is not utilized, that section reference **must not** be used for any other purpose.
- Have maps and appendices following immediately after each section, rather than separating them to a separate section or at the end.
- Start each section on a new page.
- Enter full section numbers in the upper corner of each page (in order to avoid using page numbers, which would complicate revisions).
- To indicate when a section was written or revised, enter the date at the foot of that section, and also update the Lists of Amendments to each part in order to facilitate identification and dating of revisions.
- Number all projects.
- Provide references at the end of each part, as well as in the bibliography.

Chapter 6

MAINTENANCE PROGRAMME

6.1 INTRODUCTION

Maintenance should use natural forces to enhance the beauty of the cultural resource, but over-maintenance can destroy its beauty. Maintenance planning is an art which needs cultural and ecological sensitivity. Climate and the causes of decay control the appropriate degree of maintenance, together with the users' needs, but maintenance policies and programmes should also take into account the specific nature of every culture, aiming at a balance with natural forces.

❑ *The maintenance programme is aimed at keeping the cultural resources in a manner that will prevent the loss of any part of them. It concerns all practical and technical measures that should be taken to maintain the site in proper order. It is a continuous process, not a product.*

A maintenance programme should follow well-established cycles describing who does what work, how this work is done, and how frequently. It should describe the actions in simple terms that can be implemented by cleaners, craftspersons, supervisors and all other individuals involved in the upkeep of the cultural resource.

The implementation of the maintenance programme is followed by its re-evaluation based on results and time expended. Detailed descriptions of accurate hours worked and materials used are essential; travelling time should be kept entirely separate. Tasks should be clearly described so that outside workers can bring all the necessary tools and consumable supplies to the site, avoiding time wasted on abortive journeys.

6.2 PREVENTIVE MAINTENANCE

❑ *Prevention is the highest form of conservation. If causes of decay can be removed, or at least reduced, something worthwhile has been achieved.*

Sources of atmospheric pollution and traffic vibration can be reduced or eliminated by town planning and governmental measures. Maintenance and precautions against the hazards and risks of natural disasters can go a long way towards reducing damage to cultural resources.

❑ *Administrative procedures and rehearsals of disaster drills reduce confusion and lead to the implementation of well-tested plans.*

❑ *Documentation is an essential aspect of preventive maintenance in its widest interpretation.*

❑ *Accountancy procedures, which identify recurring trouble spots in maintenance work, contribute to preventive maintenance, allowing the causes of the trouble to be identified and corrected.*

❑ *Wherever possible, maintenance tasks should be integrated into* **a scheduled routine.**

A scheduled routine would cover:
- daily tasks, including cleaning and polishing
- weekly tasks
- monthly tasks, e.g., control of plant growth on buildings and sites
- quarterly tasks
- seasonal tasks, e.g., spring and autumn
- annual tasks
- quinquennial tasks

The scheduled routine should also have flexibility, in order to allow **emergency tasks** to be tackled promptly, such as
- after heavy rain
- after high winds
- after a fire, earthquake, flood or other natural disaster

6.2.1 Professional input

A successful **maintenance strategy** requires the involvement of responsible professionals who are properly qualified to observe and diagnose causes of decay, carry out regular inspections and prepare formal reports to the Site Commission. As the World Heritage site is of the highest value, it follows that the professionals involved in its care should also be of an equally high calibre in their own fields.

Ideally, professionals should be attached on a part-time basis to the Site Commission to provide continuity. They should be given authority to implement any recommendations they might make in their **Annual Progress Reports**, as well as the right to call in outside scientific advice and to obtain second opinions.

In the implementation of maintenance actions, professionals are involved together with supervisors, craftspersons, conservators and all the general staff working under the site commission.

The professionals appointed should:

- **ensure that all signs of decay** and items needing attention are reported by all those involved in the maintenance of the site. For example, cleaners should report attacks by insects as well as leaking roofs or pipes;
- **instruct craftspersons** so that, in their zeal to do good work, they do not destroy historical evidence or materials. They must be taught to conserve, not make it "as good as new";
- **hold regular meetings** with supervisors and administrators to plan works and give advice on control of expenditure;
- **meet the Site Commission** at least quarterly, and always have access to the director;
- **be prepared to meet the public** and explain the maintenance strategy in lectures or by publishing articles; and
- **be involved in research projects** relevant to that maintenance strategy.

A good maintenance strategy can prevent a great deal of damage and decay, and thus save money. Unfortunately, it is difficult to quantify these savings, and, as a result, those administering cultural heritage too often see only the cost of the professional service and are tempted to economize unwisely in this field.

6.2.2   The context of inspecting historic buildings and sites

❑ *The initial inspection of an historic building or site is of vital importance.*

This has to embrace the whole problem as comprehensively and quickly as possible.[1]

The causes of decay – indeed, two or three causes may be operating simultaneously – are so complex that it is usual for an architect to be unaware of all but the obvious ones during the initial inspection. The role of the inspector, however, is first to record the facts and then to seek the causes.

The survey, inspection and report should take account of the building or site in its context where relevant; local planning departments can assist in preventing traffic vibrations by diverting heavy vehicles, reducing atmospheric pollution by correct siting of industries and power stations, and reducing fire hazard by considering access for fire-fighting vehicles.

❑ *The inspector should have no preconceptions about the site.*

❑ *Inspections, followed by careful research, analysis and recording, are not an end in themselves. Action must follow.*

---

1   Concerning historic buildings, suggested norms for an experienced conservation architect are 5 hours site work for a small building, 10 hours for a more complicated one and between 20 and 40 hours for a difficult or large one. Particularly complex monumental buildings, such as cathedrals, may, however, require much more time – over 1000 work-hours.

❑ *The first action should be to devise a strategic maintenance plan.*

Experience has proved that if a maintenance plan is followed for ten years, the amount of annual maintenance required decreases dramatically. Although it has been demonstrated that managing the conservation of historic sites on a preventive maintenance basis saves money, many administrators fail to understand this and are reluctant to commission regular inspections and organize a maintenance programme because of the cost of professional services and the necessary staff.

6.2.3 Monitoring a maintenance programme

Once a maintenance programme is implemented, it often takes years to work off the backlog of maintenance that is found by the first professional surveys. However, if estimates and actual costs are controlled and updated with adjustments for inflation and other variations, the eventual total cost incurred will be lower than the sum of a series of *ad hoc* responses.

Accounting systems should be designed to assist cost monitoring. It will be necessary for all concerned to keep weekly time sheets and to use the correct categories and descriptions of the work they have executed. Supervisors should check and countersign time sheets, look for any discrepancies and prevent waste or theft of materials, they should also set work targets for each staff member, and compare the actual costs of time and materials with estimated costs.

❑ *Good management and supervision are essential for maintenance work where individuals are dispersed and tackling a wide range of tasks. Craftspersons and conservators involved in these tasks must understand the basis of their work.*

6.3   SPECIAL PROBLEMS

6.3.1   Vandalism and theft

At the 1851 Great Exhibition in London, there were no problems arising from public behaviour even though diamonds were displayed without protection! It seems that public respect for cultural property has deteriorated seriously over the last hundred years; this is probably due, in part, to the impact of tourism, although there are great variations between nations and cultures in this respect.

All staff members and the public must be made aware of their duty to hinder vandalism and theft and to report any incident immediately. Uniformed staff should be able to identify any potential vandals and approach them in a positive way, asking if they can explain anything of interest in the site, so countering the blind ignorance and undirected energy that is often the cause of vandalism. Other potentially dangerous activities, such as wandering into restricted areas to pick wild flowers or lighting picnic fires, should be prevented by introductory lectures and circulation of suitable codes of behaviour. In buildings, vandalism and theft can be reduced or eliminated by the use of television cameras that can record under very low ambient light conditions using infra-red. Radio links between staff and the control centre enable the actions of a suspect to be monitored effectively.

The theft of art and archaeological material has become a major international industry. Experience shows that none of numerous sophisticated systems devised to prevent it are absolute. Since thieves are concerned about their getaway, the control of site access and the prohibition of vehicles near sensitive spots assists in security. Security is the responsibility of the site managers and should not be left only to hired guards who will merely cause security costs to escalate. Specialist advice is desirable, however, but it should be considered together with the needs of fire protection and the safety of the occupants of buildings.

6.3.2   Fire detection and protection

Fires caused by humans are usually preventable. Forest fires, however, are another matter and require careful consideration. Lightning could be a major hazard if a proper protection system is not installed and maintained annually. The destruction of irreplaceable cultural property by fire should be prevented through the introduction of such measures as taking appropriate security precautions to reduce the risk of arson, and prohibiting smoking except in designated areas.

One of the worst fire hazards is faulty electrical installation. The electrical installation should be tested at yearly intervals and will probably need renewal if it is over twenty years old; it may be possible to re-plan it in such a way that only essential services are kept live at night.

Fire-detection systems are set off by the presence of flame, smoke or heat. Since they can be subject to frequent false alarms, sensors should be wired together, so that if one fails there is no false alarm, and two are activated if there is a fire. Generally, fire-detection systems are designed for commercial buildings and their performance may be limited in historic buildings, so management should be aware of their limitations. If possible, two independent systems should be installed, since one of them might fail at the vital moment. It is advisable to link the detection system directly to the fire station. Hand extinguishers (powder or appropriate type of gas – such as CO_2 – are safest for cultural property), hose reels and fire hydrants should be carefully located on the site, and clearly signposted. Local sources of water for firefighting should be identified and recorded.

It is imperative that **all** staff receive basic training in fire prevention, fire fighting and first aid, with regular drills in work hours to practice emergency procedures. A Fire Prevention Officer should be appointed by the Director.

If a fire cannot be controlled in three minutes, it may be a total disaster in five minutes. This means that, in the case of remote historic buildings, it is desirable to install an automatic fire protection system, which at least will prevent a total loss. The experience gained in Norway, Japan and the United Kingdom could provide valuable guidance (see Fire Protection Association, no date; and Larsen and Marstein, 1992, in the bibliography).

Automatic gas and water-sprinkler fire protection systems are a good investment, but like all modern technical apparatus, their design requires sensitivity when they are to be installed in historic buildings. Previously, Halon gas systems, although expensive, were considered the best form of protection, as low concentrations do not directly endanger human life or cultural property. It has recently been realized, however, that these gases destroy the earth's protective ozone layer, and so should not be used. The problem with sprinklers is that water usually damages the building and often leaves behind it the threat of fungal attack to its fabric and contents. Whether using gas or water, it is essential to eliminate false alarms to avoid costly waste of gas or damage to the cultural resource.

❑ *Staff practices in fire drills and using fire extinguishers are essential and the fire-fighting corps should also make practice runs at least once a year and be provided with special entry and control points.*

❑ *In the case of an historic town, there should be a strategic fire-fighting plan allowing duplicate access to all buildings in case one way is blocked, and ensuring sufficient supplies of water for fire fighting.*

Practice runs will show up weaknesses which can then be corrected. Access for fire fighting must be planned and improved in order to allow heavy fire engines to reach key points. A copious supply of water from hydrants, tanks or other sources must be ensured.

Passive fire protection – such as fire-resisting doors (closed at night but not locked), fireproof partitions and sub-divisions of roof spaces – is always on duty and helps to limit the spread of fire. On natural sites, fire breaks come into this category.

Chapter 7

STAFFING AND PERSONNEL SERVICES

7.1   SITE COMMISSION

The world's cultural property can be saved and properly maintained only if adequate numbers of properly trained personnel – starting at the highest political or administrative levels down to craftspersons, site supervisors, guardians and guides – are available at the site. In addition, it has been recommended that a commission, which would function as the guardian of sites belonging to the world cultural heritage, be established for each site or group of sites. The professional and administrative structure of this Site Commission may vary according to the situation in each country or the character of the site, but its members should be experienced specialists from various professions (architects, archaeologists, planners, lawyers, etc.). Also, it is in the interest of the World Heritage site that the Site Commission's relation to the national government should be such that it has sufficient freedom of action. The Site Commission should maintain close contact with the World Heritage Committee, which can offer it support when required.

❑   *The role of the Site Commission involves informing the public of the importance of the World Heritage site, whether it be an isolated monument, historic building, historic city nucleus or industrial complex. Its duty is to accept and apply international conventions and charters while taking into consideration local and internal laws and customs, determine and oversee the implementation of the most acceptable ways of maintaining, using and protecting the site under its control.*

When it comes to World Heritage sites, local interests are frequently opposed to national and international aims. The Site Commission's responsibility is to reconcile the legitimate interests of the local inhabitants with those of the visitors who come to their site. One of the most important issues to be addressed is the level of tourism: intensive tourism can upset the lives of the local population and provoke the devaluation, or even the collapse, of their culture.

7.2   STAFFING FOR GENERAL MANAGEMENT

7.2.1   Selection of experts and professionals

The list of professionals who might be involved to a greater or lesser extent in the management of cultural heritage is a long one.

- administrators
- anthropologists
- antiquarians
- archaeologists
- architects
- architectural conservators
- archivists
- art historians
- biologists
- botanists
- building surveyors
- chemists
- conservators (of collections)
- craftspersons
- curators
- documentalists
- ecologists
- economic historians
- engineers (all sorts)
- entomologists
- ethnologists
- geographers
- geologists
- heritage recorders
- historians
- hydrologists
- landscape architects
- legislators
- mineralogists
- museologists
- petrologists
- politicians
- property managers
- seismologists
- sociologists
- surveyors

The list above is by no means complete. It indicates, however, the range of skills involved and demonstrates to young persons that there are opportunities in the developing field of conservation of cultural property.

❑   *As so many disciplines are involved, it is essential that there be clear concepts to guide practice, which entails the application of manual skills and scientific knowledge, together with artistic and historical sensitivity, which comes from cultural preparation. Without well-defined concepts, conservation will fail in its objectives.*

The selection of experts can be difficult. Learned societies or professional institutions are one source of names. It is recommended that experts should serve for at least seven years to ensure continuity, and no more than twelve years unless an awareness of new thinking and practice is demonstrated. As in the field of medicine, the conservation expert should always agree to receive a second, or even a third, independent opinion.

7.2.2 Staffing requirements

Staffing requirements must be assessed when the size of the tasks in each area of skill has been defined. The budget for salaries should be established on the basis of local experience and national grades. In some countries the scale of remuneration is unrealistically low and staff-members are often attracted by higher pay in industry or commerce.

❑ *The Site Commission should establish its own salary grades. Skilled craftspersons should be graded as technicians, not as building operatives. There should be an agreement with the State Party to review the funds available for salaries at regular intervals because needs may expand and new fields of activity be developed.*

It is best to start by appointing key personnel and then adding support as necessary. Initially staff can be given fixed-term contracts for a probationary period, followed by firm appointments where appropriate.

Many governments may want to manage the site directly for reasons of political prestige and patronage during their term of government. This can act against the interests of interpreting the inherent cultural values of the site, since their approach may lack the sensitivity and flexibility and speed of decision-making that can be the hallmark of a well constituted Site Commission at arm's length from government. This is not to deny the government's legitimate interest in the management of the site, for it will be responsible for appointing the members of the Site Commission and renewing their appointments in due course.

7.2.3 Need for qualified personnel

The need for qualified personnel ought to be self-evident when considering that a World Heritage site is truly irreplaceable. Although monetary values should not be taken as an absolute criterion, the cost of saving cultural resources from decay and destruction can be seen in better proportion when the cost of a replacement is considered.

Administrators in the field of conservation should possess a special understanding of the strengths and weaknesses of different types of personnel engaged in conservation activities. One aspect of administration which leads to totally disproportionate frustration on the part of conservators are the obstacles in their way to obtaining small amounts of special products and services. These controls may be necessary for political or economic reasons when dealing with large sums of money but, in the interest of efficiency, conservators should be allowed to purchase these small amounts by direct order as there is often only one supplier in the world. The difference is not only in time – say 1 month against 2 years – but also in terms of the damage that may occur during the delay. The cost of producing the paperwork to process such small requests often considerably exceeds the cost of the item itself.

❏ *Delays in decision-making lead to inefficiency and cost money because the decay of the cultural resource continues and usually accelerates, sometimes dramatically with time. The Site Commission and the Director must work together to minimize administrative delays.*

7.2.4   The role of conservation crafts

The scope of building craft skills in conservation ranges from the simple repair and maintenance of domestic properties to the most complicated work requiring highly specialized skills. Those who carry out such specialized tasks should be classified as conservation technicians, and have a status equal to that of other professionals engaged in conservation. The clock cannot be put back and the extreme diversification of eighteenth- and nineteenth-century crafts cannot be recreated artificially.

However, a young but sufficiently experienced tradesperson can acquire additional skills, and with artistic guidance, skilled application and the help of science it is possible to repair and reproduce the craftsmanship of the past.

❏ *In fact, skills are gained by time, experience and training. Guidance by trade masters is essential to ensure continuity; site workshops can promote this. Conservation craftspersons should understand the history of technology of their craft and be able to analyse how historic work was set out and produced. Samples of past workmanship should be collected and used for reference (as is done in Amsterdam, The Netherlands, and at Torun, Poland).*

7.2.5   Good workmanship

Good workmanship depends partly upon proper pay for a fair day's work. Overtime and the piece-working of production have led to bad workmanship and should not be used to obtain increased output when dealing with World Heritage sites.

Good workmanship is the result of proper training, continuity of work, appreciation and respect for the status of the worker. Craftspersons are primarily responsible for the quality of workmanship. Unfortunately, the present-day building industry has different objectives from the past, emphasizing quantity and often neglecting the proper use of craft skills.

The ability to evaluate quality of workmanship depends upon experience obtained only from inspecting many buildings of different periods. The Site Commission should examine the possibility of a specialized labour force for the Site with proper project and budgetary control; it may be possible to produce higher quality workmanship more economically.

7.3 EXAMPLES OF CONSERVATION SKILLS

The conservation professionals involved in the treatment of World Heritage sites are many, but some comments are offered on the following key groups:
- conservation architects and their teams of co-workers;
- architectural conservators;
- art and archaeological conservators; and
- heritage recorders.

Most professionals working in architectural conservation are used to teamwork and making the most of compromises. In addition they should possess an awareness of history, especially the history of styles and technology, as well as an understanding of the role of the craftsperson, the art historian and archaeologist.

7.3.1 Conservation architects and their teams of co-workers

Conservation architects – known also as historical architects or preservation architects – should possess basic and practical experience as general architects, as well as a knowledge and understanding of early building technology and the ability to identify and interpret a building's original fabric and later additions. They must also be able to coordinate the work of archaeologists, historians, engineers, planners, landscape architects, contractors, suppliers, conservation craftspersons, conservators and others who might be involved in a conservation project.

The **conservation architect** is the generalist in the whole building conservation process. He or she should possess a good knowledge of all periods of architecture, combined with a thorough understanding of contemporary building practice; this is critical to the evaluation and preservation of the artistic and historical value of the site, where contemporary requirements must also be met. This includes complying with relevant codes of practice and building regulations, or obtaining waivers to any inapplicable building-code regulations where justified by reference to fundamental principles. In addition to a knowledge of building technology, an understanding of the pathology of buildings (such as causes of sinking foundations, crumbling walls and rotting timbers) is essential.

It is hoped that more **building contractors** will specialize in repair and maintenance and that a new breed of conservation technicians, well versed in the history of the technology of their craft, will emerge to take a place with equal status and remuneration alongside the architect. The role of **engineers**, in all specialties but especially in structural engineering, is of great importance in conservation work. Engineers have to be properly trained to understand the demands of historic fabric, and to be able to work with conservation teams. Often, more harm is done by wrong treatment (methods, materials) than by neglect.

7.3.2 Architectural conservators

The difficulty that conservation architects have in finding and communicating effectively to those scientists who are able to appreciate their problems has led the *American National Conservation Advisory Council* to recommend the recognition of a greater degree of specialization in architectural conservation. Persons with these special responsibilities would be called Architectural Conservators, and they should have a broad range of skills beyond those of either the historical architect or arts conservator.

Architectural conservators must be trained in the new technologies and scientific laboratory methods now being applied to the conservation of artefacts in other fields; they must also be able to tap resources in such sub-specialties of chemistry as spectrographic analysis, radio-carbon dating and resistivity analysis. They should know how to use new archaeological techniques for analysing site evidence; computer technology for retrieval of recorded information; and photogrammetry for producing accurate dimensional drawings and solving difficult problems of recording. Very few such persons exist at present.

7.3.3 Art and archaeological conservators

In some countries, archaeological investigation is mandatory before any interventions are carried out, and this should be the case for World Heritage sites. Art and archaeological conservators require good manual skills, a training in art history and some training in the sciences, but above all a discerning eye. This contribution of skills is rare, as the educational system does not produce this hybrid cross of the sciences and humanities. Manual dexterity is essential but an academic degree is a good starting point whether it be in art history, archaeology or anthropology. Still, in each case something has to be added.

Art and archaeological conservators receive academic training at a university; although this should develop their intellectual ability, it does not teach administration, cooperation or teamwork. It would help if the history of their subject were considered, as this would give a valuable sense of proportion and a knowledge of new ideas which might affect long-term planning in their field. There are a few specialist courses for conservators and these are listed in the ICCROM *Training Directory*. It takes a great deal of training, including a range of field and site experience, to produce a conservator with the wide range of skills required. Theory and academic qualifications are not enough.

7.3.4 Heritage recorders

Heritage recording and documentation has developed into a specialized profession in many countries. Although conservators may be involved in carrying out site recording and documentation, as well as reporting on inspections and surveys, the complexity of an accurate and rationally managed recording process has led to the need for specialized heritage recorders. They should be able to read and understand the character and values of heritage sites in order to document them properly. In addition, they should be aware of current standards of documentation and be able to master relevant technologies, develop links with documentation centres and work in close collaboration with other heritage conservators according to common objectives.

7.4   RECRUITMENT AND CAREERS

Recruitment into the whole field of conservation generally comes after a first academic degree, but technicians and craftspersons should also be admitted if they have the necessary potential and are prepared to study. Distance learning training courses – such as those of the Open University in the United Kingdom – could widen the number of entrants.

Although there are vast, still-unquantified amounts of conservation work to be done (250 work-years was an estimate for just one national museum), some conservators have no work because of lack of funds and some work is not commissioned because the appropriate conservator cannot be found. This confused situation arises because governments (with some notable exceptions, such as Poland) have not addressed the question of financing conservation, and a career structure for conservators has not developed. As it takes at least twenty years for a conservation service to become truly operational, it is advisable to set up a central committee, such as the *United States Advisory Committee for Conservation,* to guide progress. The former Soviet Union had an interesting career structure for both academics and artisans in the conservation field.

Conservators should rank equal with the museum curator or keeper and, if interested in management, should have an equal opportunity to fill directorial posts; such is the case in the United Kingdom. The challenges produced by the need to manage World Heritage sites should stimulate States Parties to review the whole question of recruitment and careers in conservation. Normal procedures should apply to appointments. Practical ability, initiative and an ability to improvise should rank highly.

7.5   CONSERVATION FACILITIES

To make conservation function properly, various grades of employment and varying degrees of support are necessary.[1]

There is a need to establish appropriate **documentation centres**, such as libraries and archives, which can hold source material and records. In addition, facilities are

---

1   For a discussion of this, see: R.M. Organ, in the bibliography.

required for producing photographic or photogrammetric records and measured drawings (from hand drawings to CAD and image processing techniques). While larger sites often need to operate their own recording units, centralized units and photogrammetry laboratories may also be used.

Conservation facilities for the scientific research and treatment of heritage resources can be categorized in terms of their performance and described in a series in which specific functions vary according to the tasks of the conservation professionals they serve: craftspersons, conservator-restorers, applied scientists, and research scientists.

- The **craft shop** has few functions: these may include work such as framing, matting or laminating. An object only enters the shop for a specific treatment. Examination is limited to supplying preparatory data for that treatment. In such a shop, a specific and narrow range of skills may be practised to perfection, and productivity per person can be high. The type and quality of materials used are those traditionally accepted in similar shops, but a client's special request may be satisfied for an increased fee.

  In conservation, the hand often informs the brain, so manual skills are essential, but the expertise of craftspersons, generated by years of practice and repetition, is often undervalued. It should be remembered that it is easier to acquire scientific knowledge, or to learn art history, than to become specialized in a manual skill. **The technology of the past is embodied in craft procedures, and until the rationale for these are understood it is rash to propose changes.**

- A **small conservation facility** could be served perhaps by one experienced and knowledgeable person, assisted by a few helpers who may not possess formal conservation training. A range of objects will be treated here. Examinations will be carried out to programme a type of treatment, but the principal functions will be to execute interventions based on experience. Approved materials are used, and special housekeeping procedures are imposed on the staff which handles, stores and displays the objects.

- A **facility handling a variety of objects from closely associated specific collections** will be staffed by conservator-restorers possessing experience with each category of object in these collections. Examination will be more thorough than that found in the other facilities already described, but given a base of extensive experience, most conditions can usually be recognized on sight. Occasionally, a laboratory analysis will be needed to confirm what the conservator-restorer's eye has seen. Such a facility would be fully equipped for museum-quality conservation. It could be very productive because skills would be developed from long and close experience with similar types of objects.

- The **conservation laboratory** is organized to examine in penetrating detail objects not amenable to routine treatment. Here, new procedures are devised and special materials are used to solve the particular conservation problems. This laboratory will be staffed by individuals trained in applied science and the use of complex analytical equipment. Its treatment personnel will be highly perceptive, innovative and skilled in a wide range of activities. They will not necessarily have vast experience with any one class of object, and the number of objects treated by each staff member will necessarily be small compared to the basic facilities outlined above. To allow for the treatment of difficult conservation problems, it is recommended that at least one such laboratory be established in each country.

- The last facility reflects the pure, penetrating variety of examination undertaken by research scientists, usually postgraduates in **well-equipped university departments**; they usually treat objects of assured provenance, but not necessarily of artistic quality. Such laboratories do not usually function in association with collections, but could not continue without them.

  This is the scientific complement to the art historian's stylistic study. The scientists may sometimes work with small samples provided from unobtrusive areas of valuable objects; in this situation, no treatment is given at all, nor indeed should be, unless the scientist is fully aware of the aesthetics of the object and has the needed skills. But without the basic knowledge obtained from such extensive studies, the actual conservator of a specific object might well lack the data necessary for a wise choice of methods.

With large projects involving several work-years of conservation work, a balance of personnel of several categories will be required. For example, three or four conservation craftspersons, level A, may work with a conservator-restorer, level C, advised by a research scientist, level D, and coordinated by a generalist such as a curator or an architect. Correct appraisal of the numbers of workers required at each grade is the responsibility of the conservator-restorer, and upon this will depend the efficiency of the work: a team needs a leader who can organize and ensure the correct balance of skills, working in harmony, and who is motivated by emulation rather than competition or restrictive practices.

7.6   PERSONNEL MANAGEMENT

It is essential that authority be delegated so that each level of personnel can make appropriate decisions and have the power to implement them. Yet each employee must be accountable to someone senior and this means that senior management must be professionally oriented. **Administrators are not trained to make the environmental, technical or artistic judgements that constitute the essence of conservation**. A good manager must guide the staff and permit them a say in decision-making, thus creating the high morale and job satisfaction that lead to good work.

Promotion of staff should be mainly on merit and initiative, as conservation is, or at least should be, an expanding field. Long service and concomitant experience can be rewarded by annual pay increments (over and above cost-of-living increments).

7.6.1 Contracted Services

As the scope of conservation is so wide and the required professional skills or equipment may not be available on site, it will often be necessary to contract out work to free-lance experts. It is certainly more economical to contract out operations that require sophisticated equipment which might not be needed again, could not be used regularly, or would require special staff training. It may also be necessary to contract out work because the staff are already overburdened, but they should be consulted first; otherwise, they may feel passed over and lose morale or think management has lost confidence in them (which, if true, should be discussed).

It takes great skill to frame contracts equitably. A preliminary visit by the contractor is desirable, and he or she should be invited to contribute to forming the brief. Foreign missions always present problems in communication. A trained person, ideally a former participant of an ICCROM course, or a member of the International Institute for the Conservation of History and Artistic Works (IIC), of the International Council of Museums (ICOM) or of ICOMOS, should help define the specific task which the contractor is required to deal with; this helps too in finding the right contractor for the problem.

The contractor's fee is difficult to determine because salary levels in different countries vary greatly. Contractors should be paid according to their experience and knowledge as well as their time. Rewards are both prestige and pecuniary but the former should be dominant. At least all the contractor's expenses should be paid, and he or she should not be expected to drop everything at short notice to go on an ill-prepared mission.

Some contractors are very dilatory and even irresponsible about submitting their reports, so it is wise to withhold at least one third of their fee until the report is received. After receipt of the report there should be a debriefing session with face-to-face discussion.

7.6.2 Standards and Training

Since the development of recent conservation and restoration philosophies and practices, the training and education of competent practitioners and project managers has been an important issue in development of conservation policies. A large number of training programmes were established during the 1970s and 1980s; while most of them are in Europe, many have also been initiated in other continents.

Recommendations to give proper attention to training and education have been given in many international documents, including UNESCO Recommendations and the World Heritage Convention.[2] Other international bodies have provided funds for this purpose, and there are specific commitments also at regional and national levels.

One of the most important functions of ICCROM is to focus on the development of international training programmes in the different fields of conservation and restoration of cultural heritage. Being an intergovernmental organization, ICCROM collaborates with its Member States to develop and establish appropriate training programmes in different countries and regions. It has thus obtained great experience in training in the international field and served as the model for several national courses. International meetings have also been organized by ICCROM in order to establish a worldwide network of contacts for the exchange of information and experiences in the different fields. Reports of these meetings are available from ICCROM.

The ICCROM *International Directory on Training in Conservation of Cultural Heritage,* published in collaboration first with UNESCO and then with the Getty Conservation Institute, lists all known courses in the world which have a specific conservation input, including landscape and garden conservation. Although it is essential that training programmes be tied to the national educational infrastructure, such programmes should not be developed in isolation. ICCROM can provide its Member States with advice on possible lecturers, or collaborate on short courses for specific aspects of conservation.

It should be national policy to make potential professionals (i.e., architects, archaeologists, art historians and tradespeople) aware of the significance of their own World Cultural Heritage Sites and thus to encourage interest and recruitment into the field of conservation. However, if salaries for conservation work are too far below those for work in commercial fields, it will be difficult to retain trained professionals. When government service salaries are considered too low, there is an advantage in having a site commission at arm's length from government, so that it can set salary scales that are sufficient to retain staff of the required calibre.

In training, the first priority should be to impart the principles and ethics of conservation so that professionals have standards by which to evaluate proposed actions. Second, the role of the professional should be examined and, if necessary, training in making inspections and reports should be provided. Third, the nature of materials and both traditional and present-day technology should be studied so that the appropriate solution for a project can be developed with special attention to traditional skills and materials. Finally, legislation, documentation and planning procedures should be studied.

---

2   See also the ICOMOS Training Guidelines, included as Appendix E.

Chapter 8

TREATMENTS AND AUTHENTICITY

8.1 AIM OF TREATMENTS

During the past two centuries, restoration principles have evolved into a coherent approach to the treatment and management of objects. This is especially true when one considers collections and monuments. However, the management of other types of heritage resources, such as historic ensembles, historic towns or landscapes, is more complex. Rather, one can see a convergence of principles in methodologies, and the cumulative experience is being reinforced through research, training, technical cooperation and the exchange of resource management experiences. Treatments inevitably involve some loss of certain cultural property values, but this loss can usually be justified in order to preserve the essential integrity of the cultural properties for future generations.

The treatment strategies for cultural heritage sites should be conceived according to the following principles:

They must assure reversibility, i.e.,

- if technically possible, use materials whose effect can be reversed,
- not prejudice a future intervention whenever one may become necessary,
- not hinder the possibility of later access to all evidence incorporated in the object.

They must maintain authenticity, i.e.,

- allow the maximum amount of existing historical material to be retained (authenticity in material),
- ensure harmony with original design and workmanship (in colour, tone, texture, form and scale),
- do not allow new additions to dominate over the original fabric, but respect its archaeological potential, and
- meet the test of authenticity in design, material, workmanship or setting and in the case of cultural landscapes their distinctive character and components.

8.1.1 Preparedness

The treatment of cultural heritage resources is a complex undertaking that requires expertise in the principles and international guidelines of conservation. Conservators should be thoroughly trained in the application of appropriate methods and procedures. Each conservation project should be duly studied and assessed, and its problems solved according to relevant needs and conditions. Conservators should be cautious of preconceived solutions, and the development of an appropriate treatment strategy should include examination of experiences from past treatments at the same and similar sites. The treatment should be subjected to routine monitoring in order to evaluate its effectiveness.

8.1.2   Priorities

The critical relationship of conservation objectives to resource values and the physical evaluation process will influence the formulation of treatment strategies. Considering that the most important aim of the conservation of World Heritage sites is to maintain their authenticity, it is necessary to establish a hierarchy of resource-specific concerns:

- The first priority is to establish, safeguard and maintain the **cultural values** for which a World Heritage site has been included on the List.
- All conservation treatments (e.g., protection, consolidation or restoration) should guarantee the protection of the **authenticity** of the heritage site, prolonging the duration of its integrity and preparing it for interpretation.
- Where applicable, a heritage resource should be allowed to continue to serve its traditional function, insofar as this does not cause damage to its historical integrity. If the continuity of the function is not possible, the resource should be adapted to serve an **appropriate use** as part of a carefully conceived plan that acknowledges its outstanding universal value and its educational role.

Different values often suggest different approaches to the treatment of heritage resources. Sometimes these are in conflict. Emphasis on certain values (e.g., nationalistic, educational, tourism, functional, economic or political) may lead to over-restoration, forced development and even the destruction of authenticity.

❑   *Balanced judgement, based on a hierarchy of resource values and a systematic process of evaluation, is therefore essential for the establishment of an appropriate conservation methodology and treatment strategy.*

Conservation of cultural and natural heritage is an essential part of modern socio-economic planning and development. As such it must compete with other aspects of the planning process. It is therefore essential, particularly concerning World Heritage sites, to make a realistic and critical assessment of each site in its physical, cultural and social context. This assessment must consider the resource's cultural values and the likelihood of achieving the appropriate conservation, integration and enhancement of these values in the larger socio-economic context.

8.1.3   Definition of treatment approaches

Treatment strategies range from cyclical or routine maintenance to varying degrees of consolidation, reinforcement, restoration, or even adaptive use. The appropriateness of a particular application should be justified through a critical assessment of the values involved. It is necessary to associate general concepts with specific actions in order to clarify conservation policies. The terminology used to express each type of treatment should be clarified to allow coherent communication between those involved in the conservation and management processes.

Definitions of the most commonly used conservation concepts are provided in the following sections. These are indicative rather than exact, and open to discussion.

8.1.3.1   *Protection*

Protection is understood in legal terms as the action required to provide the conditions for a monument, site or historic area to survive. The term is also related to the physical protection of historic sites to ensure their security against theft or vandalism, as well as environmental attack and visual intrusions. Buffer zones also provide protection to historic areas.

Legal protection, which is based on legislation and planning norms, aims to guarantee defence against any harmful treatment, provide guidelines for proper action, and institute corresponding punitive sanctions.

Physical protection includes the addition of roofs, shelters, coverings, etc., or even removing an endangered object to safety.

8.1.3.2   *Preservation*

Preservation aims to take the measures necessary to keep the site in its existing state. In Latin languages, the word indicates preventive action. In the United States, "historic preservation" coincides with the British usage of "conservation" in relation to historic buildings.

Preservation measures include regular inspections and cyclical and routine maintenance. It implies that repairs must be carried out as required to ensure resource integrity. In practice, this means that damage and deterioration (such as that caused by water, chemicals, insects, rodents or other pests, plants and microorganisms) must be arrested and reversed when discovered.

8.1.3.3   *Conservation*

Conservation implies keeping in safety or preserving the existing state of a heritage resource from destruction or change,[1] i.e., the action taken to prevent decay and to prolong life (Feilden, 1982: 3). The general concept of conservation implies various types of treatments aimed at safeguarding buildings, sites or historic towns; these include maintenance, repair, consolidation, reinforcement.

---

1   *The Shorter Oxford English Dictionary.*

In relation to urban areas or cultural landscapes, conservation is part of an integrated approach to management. It is necessary, therefore, to accept a degree of gradual change with due consideration to the values and authenticity for which these areas have been classified as protected zones. In the UNESCO *Recommendation concerning Safeguarding and the Contemporary Role of Historic Areas* (agreed in Nairobi, 1976), social functions and continuous use are of fundamental importance for their conservation.

Conservation is also used for the treatment of individual building elements, objects in collections and materials. In this context, conservation treatments are limited to protecting the original material, cleaning and consolidation.

The primary aim of conservation is to preserve the authenticity and integrity of the cultural resource.

8.1.3.4   *Consolidation*

Consolidation is the physical addition or application of adhesive or supportive materials to the actual fabric of the cultural property in order to ensure its continued durability or structural integrity.

Consolidation treatments can have a negative impact if not carried out with a clear understanding of the short-term and long-term physical implications of treatment, the likelihood of changes in the original object and the principle of reversibility.

8.1.3.5   *Restoration*

Restoration has had several meanings in the past; the most commonly accepted definition was to return to an object its lost form or appearance.[2] In North America, the term is often linked to "period restoration," i.e., the re-creation of the aesthetic design concept of a building in a given period. In England, 'restoration' was considered as a negative or destructive treatment, following the debates led by John Ruskin during the second half of the nineteenth century. In Latin languages, 'restoration' has often been used as a general term related to the conservation of the built cultural heritage.

Today, however, restoration has been given a specific definition, as expressed in Articles 9-13 of the Venice Charter. The aim of restoration is not only to conserve the integrity of the resource, but also to reveal its cultural values and to improve the legibility of its original design. Restoration is a highly specialized operation based on a critical-historical process of evaluation, and must not be based on conjecture. The aim of modern restoration – to reveal the original state within the limits of still existing material – thus differs from the past aim of bringing back the original by rebuilding a lost form. The French term *mise-en-valeur* is closely linked to this notion.

---

2   "To bring back to the original state," *Ibid.*

8.1.3.6 *Reconstruction*

Reconstruction means building anew.[3] The term may be used in reference to work executed, using modern or old material, or both, with the aim of rebuilding dismembered or destroyed elements, or parts of them. Reconstruction must be based on accurate archaeological and architectural documentation and evidence, never on conjecture.

Although reconstruction may prove to be an appropriate strategy following disasters such as fire, earthquake or war, its validity is more questionable when it is used as a measure to improve the presentation of heritage sites. The relocation of a monument or part of it to a new site would also require reconstruction; this might be justified when deemed necessary in order to protect a resource from environmental hazards such as flooding and pollution. The moving of a resource from the original site should not be allowed except "where it is justified by national or international interests of paramount importance."[4]

8.1.3.7 *Anastylosis*

Anastylosis, the Greek for 'restoration' or 're-erection of columns,' has come to mean "the re-assembling of existing but dismembered parts."[5] Anastylosis is generally used when referring to structures consisting of clearly identifiable components, such as dry masonry or timber,[6] and not to monolithic structures such as brick walls with mortar.

Anastylosis is a type of 'restoration'; it aims to make the spatial character of a ruined structure visually more comprehensible by reinstating its lost original form, using the original material that is both in suitable condition and is located at the site. The work must be guided on the basis of the same rules as restoration and supported by firm archaeological evidence. Generally this is the only form of reconstruction acceptable on World Heritage sites.

8.1.4 Treatments and architecture

Architecture involves dealing with materials that accommodate functional use and is subject to environmental variables. A building has to function first of all as a viable structure, resisting static and dynamic loads. It must also incorporate an internal environment that is appropriate for the programmed usage, and it must be protected against hazards such as fire and vandalism, winds, floods and

---

3   *ibid.*
4   *Venice Charter*, Art. 7.
5   *Venice Charter*, Art. 15 – Excavations.
6   The definition of *anastylosis* refers mainly to blocks of stone (e.g., the restoration of Greek temples), but anastylosis of timber structures (e.g., the restoration of oriental temples) is also valid.

earthquakes. In addition to these concerns involving the building fabric, conservation of a heritage resource also involves attention to issues related to the preservation of its site, its setting and its physical environment.

❑ *Preventive maintenance should in most cases forestall the need for major interventions, and it has been well documented that good maintenance reduces the cost of conservation of historic resources.*

The conservation of the cultural heritage resources is a significant cultural challenge. This is in part due to the scale and complexity of the issues involved, as well as the involvement of many different professions. Conservation activities do not follow a simple formula; rather, they depend on an appropriate understanding of the values of the heritage resource.

The policy of conservation involves making interventions at various scales and levels of intensity.

❑ *The prescribed actions are determined by the physical condition, the causes of deterioration and the anticipated future environment of the individual cultural resource.*

While specific symptoms and associated problems must be addressed, each resource must always be considered as a whole, taking into account a full range of factors in the prescription of preservation treatments.

Decisions concerning the treatment of World Heritage sites must be based on the balanced judgements of a multidisciplinary team. The objectives of the Convention serve as a reference in establishing priority goals and recommendations, and the final management objectives and the general principles of good conservation and restoration practice must be kept in mind, namely:

- understanding the objectives,
- communicating the prescribed tasks, and
- supervising their implementation.

Remember that a policy of minimum intervention has generally proven to be the best policy for ensuring effective conservation, and that the best way of preserving buildings or sites (as opposed to museum collections) is to keep them in use. The original type of use is generally the best, since it implies fewer changes to the whole of the building. When this is not feasible, appropriate new uses that are compatible with the design and associated values of the building or site may be proposed; this practice may involve what is called *mise-en-valeur,* or modernization with or without adaptive alteration.

The conversion of the heritage resource to suit a new use (such as adapting a mediaeval convent in Venice to house a school and laboratory for stone conservation, or turning an eighteenth-century barn into a domestic dwelling), is sometimes the only economically viable way that historical and aesthetic values can be saved and historic buildings and sites can be brought up to contemporary life, safety and functional standards.

Converting an historic building for **museum** purposes (e.g., to display collections or to serve as a house museum), also implies giving it a new use; this may often require transformations in order accommodate large numbers of visitors while ensuring adequate security and meeting the prescribed standards for environment, lighting, fire safety, access, services, etc.

The question of new uses is particularly relevant to historic urban areas, in which difficult social and economic problems related to the management and control of rehabilitation must be addressed. To transform an historic town into a museum or to use it as a hotel or tourist residence would obviously completely change its original social functions, giving it a new and different character. While such use may sometimes be a reasonable solution, keeping or reviving the original types of compatible social functions should be given high priority.

8.1.5   Treatments and ruins

❏   *A site in ruins can be defined as a construction that has lost so much of its original form and substance that its potential unity as a functional structural form is also gone.*[7]

The ruined state, however, may possess significance and represent specific cultural values. Because of their lost physical integrity, historic ruins are subject to particular problems of decay, and therefore merit special treatment and care. Even in the case of relatively simple physical features without complex ornamental or structural characteristics, the appropriateness of conservation or restoration treatments and the quality of workmanship in repairs will determine the success of the end result.

The extent and the location of any new work must be carefully considered, since it may have a significant effect on the historical character of the site. Even when these interventions are aimed at the stabilization, protection, or interpretation of the ruins, the issue of new construction is often controversial, and requires both a sensitive and sensible consideration of conservation objectives.

❏   *The primary purpose of the treatment of World Heritage ruins is to safeguard the historic substance and present it to the public.*

---

7   "That which remains after decay and fall." "The remains of a decayed and fallen building or town." *Shorter Oxford English Dictionary.*

The interpretation and evaluation of ruins depends on the quality, location and extent of the losses of material and structural integrity, on the knowledge and reliable documentation of lost features, and on the cultural significance of the ruined state in the definition of the monument and its setting.

Anastylosis should be considered only if original elements still exist on the site in sufficiently pristine condition to justify it, and if the work to be undertaken will not unbalance the overall setting and the values of the heritage resource. An historic site with its setting may possess an important archaeological potential. On the other hand, the relationship of the site to the contemporary social and economic context may override cultural values, and thus justify adaptive uses and treatments.

However, there must be awareness of the danger that such action may compromise, or in extreme cases destroy, its status as a World Heritage site.

8.2   HOW DOES TREATMENT RELATE TO AUTHENTICITY ?

According to the principles of the *World Heritage Convention* (art. 4) the primary aim of cultural resource management is to guarantee that the values for which the site has been listed are maintained and appropriately presented to the general public. A comprehensive maintenance strategy that includes regular inspections is necessary to achieve this objective. The designation of the resource as a World Heritage site in itself exacerbates management pressures due to increased tourism, which can accelerate wear and tear and introduce commercial activities which can be destructive or undesirable. Designation may also lead to ill-conceived proposals for restoration, anastylosis or even reconstructions stimulated by either political or commercial motives. Great caution in site management is therefore essential, and care must be taken that all action be carefully considered according to the requirements of the Convention.

According to the *Operational Guidelines* of the Convention, a monument or site that is nominated to the World Heritage List must meet the criteria of authenticity in relation to design, workmanship, material and setting. A strategy must be presented for conserving the significant values of the resource. Thus, it follows that any treatment that is planned for a monument or site on the List should recognize these criteria. The following summary briefly characterizes those aspects of the cultural resource that relate to its different forms of authenticity and appropriate conservation actions. It is emphasized, however, that while the aspects are here presented separately, care should be taken to guarantee a balanced judgement in treatments in order to maintain the authenticity as well as the historic character and significance of the heritage resource.

Authenticity in materials:

Evidence: Original building material, historical stratigraphy, evidence and marks made by impact of significant phases in history, and the process of ageing (patina of age).

Aim of treatment:	To respect historic material, to distinguish new material from historic so as not to fake or to mislead the observer; in historic areas or towns, material should be understood as referring to the physical structures, the fabric of which the area consists.
Implementation:	Maintenance and conservation of material substance related to periods of construction. In historic areas or towns this would mean maintaining the historic fabric, and avoiding replacement of even the oldest structures so far as these form the historical continuity of the area.

Authenticity in workmanship:

Evidence:	Substance and signs of original building technology and techniques of treatment in historic structures and materials.
Aim of treatment:	To respect evidence of original workmanship in building materials and structural systems.
Implementation:	Conservation and maintenance of original material and structures, with creation of harmony between repairs and eventual new parts by using traditional workmanship.

Authenticity in design:

Evidence:	Elements or aspects in which the artistic, architectural, engineering or functional design of the heritage resource and its setting are manifest (the original meaning and message, the artistic and functional idea, the commemorative aspect). In historic sites, areas or landscapes, design should be referred to the larger context as relevant to each case.
Aim of treatment:	To respect the design conception as expressed and documented in the historic forms of the original structure, architecture, urban or rural complex.
Implementation:	Conservation, maintenance, repair, consolidation, restoration or anastylosis of historic structures, and harmonization of any eventual new constructions with the design conceptions expressed in historic forms.

Authenticity in setting:

Evidence:	The site or setting of the resource related to the periods of construction; historic park or garden; historic or cultural landscape; townscape value; and group value.

| *Aim of* | To keep the heritage resource *in situ* in its original site, and to |
| *treatment:* | maintain the relationship of the site to its surroundings; |

Implementation: Planning control, urban or territorial conservation planning, and integrated conservation.

While the questions of authenticity and appropriate treatments mentioned here are mainly conceived in relation to historic structures, it is necessary to give serious consideration to traditional settlements especially in rural areas, such as villages and cultural landscapes characterized by traditional forms of life and functions, including gradual change and construction activities. In such cases, the continuation of traditional crafts and skills may be an essential part of the relevant management policy in order to guarantee coherence within a traditional economic system, life style and habitat. Attention should be paid to ensuring genuine quality in such crafts, and avoiding substitution with industrial products or methods. Furthermore, experience has shown that traditional types of materials should generally be recommended, especially when new paint, mortar, etc., need to be applied, in order to guarantee physical and aesthetic coherence with the existing structure.

8.2.1   Treatments related to authenticity in material

Authenticity in material is based on values associated with the physical substance of the **original heritage resource**. Emphasis should be given to the protection, conservation and maintenance of the original fabric – whether related to a single building or historic area.

❑ *The aim of treatment is to prolong the life-span of original materials and structures, to keep them in their original position in the construction and on the site (in situ), to preserve the age value and the patina of age of the resource, and to retain the traces of its history, use or changes over time.*

The question of material authenticity in relation to plants and historic gardens requires a different specification, because plants are living and dynamic entities, with a natural cycle of growth, decay and death. Therefore they need to be replaced at variably long intervals. With care, the original plants can be maintained for as long as possible, and replacements can be propagated from the same genetic stock. This is one way of maintaining authenticity. However, problems of competition between plants as they mature may require moving some to another position.

In fact, in the case of gardens, the question raised should be of their integrity, and whether or not this integrity exists, and what actions are considered feasible to maintain a proper balance with the historic features of the garden. An important decision that has to be made regarding conservation policy for all or part of a garden is whether a particular point in the cycle of growth is selected as the point of reference, or whether one accepts that they must complete all or part of the cycle before replacement. These decisions must be made in the context of the particular garden. Authenticity should be referred mainly to the physical layout and features of non-organic materials.

Preventive action includes the provision of regular maintenance and making necessary repairs before damage occurs. It also implies anticipating potential threats and, by planning and direct intervention, so prevent damage. In the case of a ruin that has lost its protective envelope, weathering and decay is exacerbated; protective action may, therefore, include covers or roofs to shelter fragile or endangered parts. This must be carried out unobtrusively and with sensitivity towards the character of the monument and the values of the site. An extreme action could be removing decorative parts from the monument in order to conserve them in a museum; such action should be considered temporary, and it is advisable only if no other means of protection are available. It is, in fact, in conflict with the principle of keeping historically significant material in its original context.

Replacement of original elements. Once material has been cut and used in a construction, it has become historic and is linked with the historical time line of the object. Although restoration by replacement of decayed materials and structural elements will reduce material authenticity in the monument, it can be acceptable within the limits of potential unity if it is vital for the survival of the remaining original structure. When appropriately executed with similar materials and workmanship, the result should be compatible with the original character of the structure. The replacement of original elements should be strictly limited in extent, and carried out in a way that it does not diminish the value of the original substance.

Consolidation and reinforcement. When the strength of materials or structural elements is reduced to the extent that it can no longer survive anticipated threats, consolidation or reinforcement may be advisable. Such treatment will, however, reduce the authenticity of the resource because the original substance is altered. The combination of traditional materials and modern industrial products can be incompatible. The use of modern industrial products for the consolidation of traditional building materials can physically or chemically transform the original to the extent that its material authenticity may be lost, although the appearance may still be the same. Such treatments should be decided only after a careful, critical assessment of the implications in each case. One should also keep in mind that treatments such as injections and grouting may be difficult or impossible to reverse if they are unsuccessful. Prior to undertaking such interventions, a proper balance between protection and consolidation should be found through careful scientific analyses of the character and consistency of the original material, the environmental context and the proposed cure. In no event should historical evidence be destroyed.

❏ *The treatment itself should be properly tested for effectiveness, and its appropriateness for the material in question must be* **proven over an extended test period** *before embarking on large-scale application.*

The testing period must be long, since failures sometimes occur even after ten or fifteen years. It is important to keep an accurate record of all treatments in historic buildings and ancient monuments, and to make regular inspections of their behaviour, followed up by written reports. Research on conservation treatments should refer to these historical records.

Concerning the fabric of an historic area, one should carefully identify and define what should be conserved in order not to lose authenticity. The historical value of towns or traditional settlements lies in their structures and fabric. Therefore, conserving only fronts or elevations of historic buildings, and replacing the fabric with new constructions means a loss of authenticity and historical continuity. The aim should be conservative rehabilitation of the original fabric whenever possible.

8.2.2   Treatments related to authenticity in workmanship

Authenticity in workmanship is related to material authenticity, but its emphasis is on keeping evidence of the workmanship of the construction. It therefore draws on the archaeological potential of the monument as a testimony to these techniques.

❑   *The aim of treatment is to prolong the life-span of any materials or elements that exhibit the evidence of workmanship, and to guarantee that this is not falsified by contemporary interventions.*

Conservation. The value of authenticity in workmanship is best understood through a systematic identification, documentation and analysis of the historic production and treatment of building materials and methods of construction. This research will provide a necessary reference for the compatibility of modern conservation treatments.

Consolidation. In the case of structural consolidation or reinforcement, the integrity of the historical structural system must be respected and its form preserved. Only by first understanding how an historic building acts as a whole – that is, as a "structural-spatial environmental system" (Feilden, 1982) – is it possible to introduce appropriate new techniques, provide suitable environmental adjustments or devise sensitive adaptive uses.

Maintenance. The repair of heritage resources using compatible traditional skills and materials is of prime importance. Where traditional methods are inadequate, however, the conservation of cultural property can be achieved by the use of modern techniques. These should be reversible, proven by experience and appropriate for the scale of the project and its climatic environment.

In the case of **vernacular architecture**, which often consists of short-lived or vulnerable materials (such as reeds, mud, rammed earth, unbaked bricks and wood), the same types of materials and traditional skills should be used for the repair or restoration of worn or decayed parts. The preservation of design intentions and details is just as important as the preservation of original materials. In many cases, it is advisable to use temporary measures in the hope that some better technique will be developed, especially if consolidation would diminish resource integrity and prejudice future conservation efforts.

8.2.3   Treatments related to authenticity in design

Authenticity in design is related to the architectural, artistic, engineering and functional design of the monument, site or landscape, and the relevant setting. The commemorative value of a monument is also related to the authenticity of its design, and depends on the legibility of this intent.

❑   *The aim is to preserve original material and structures in which the design is manifest, and, when feasible, to carry out restorations or other appropriate treatments that will reveal historic forms or structures associated with relevant values that have been obscured through alterations, neglect or destruction.*

Historical stratigraphy. A restoration aimed at the recreation or reconstruction of the object in a form (style) that existed previously but has been lost would presuppose that time is reversible; the result would be a fantasy, and is referred to as stylistic restoration. This approach implies the elimination of parts relating to specific periods of history. Although stylistic restoration was considered an acceptable practice in the past, contemporary restoration strategies should be based on the condition of the resource at the present moment, so that the valid contributions and additions of all periods of its historical time line are acknowledged. Systematic survey, recording, and documentation are necessary for an assessment of the physical condition of the resource and the evaluation of its integrity as a whole and in its parts (Brandi, 1963). In relation to historic gardens or landscapes, the retention and sensitive management of historic plant material is indispensable.

In the case of **superimposed historical phases of development**, underlying layers in the historical stratigraphy of a resource can be displayed for the purpose of study and documentation. Any display of earlier phases should be discreet, and carried out in a manner that does not undermine their contributing values and conservation. Removal of elements representing the historical phases of a monument should only be carried out in exceptional circumstances, such as "when what is removed is of little interest and the material which is brought to light is of great historical, archaeological or aesthetic value, and its state of preservation good enough to justify the action."[8] These are hard conditions to satisfy.

Modern **re-integration**, or the filling of lost parts (*lacunae*) is generally acceptable so long as a potential unity exists and provides a sound basis for the operation. Treatment of lacunae is based on an evaluation of their context, and they should be reintegrated on the basis of factual evidence. If the re-integration does not

---

8   *Venice Charter*, Art. 11.

enhance the potential unity of the whole, or if the lacunae cannot be re-integrated due to the extent, position, or the artistic character of losses, then this action would not be appropriate.[9] If the losses can be re-integrated in an appropriate manner, however, treatment should be carried out following international guidelines.[10]

Although the aim of re-integration in historic buildings or other resources is to establish harmony with the original design in terms of its colour, texture and form, any replacement should at the same time be distinguishable from the original so that restoration does not falsify the artistic or historic evidence.[11] In differentiating new elements from old, care should be taken to ensure that their contrast is not excessive. The aim is to indicate the distinction, not to emphasize the difference between new and old. In addition, the extent of new parts should be small relative to the original fabric.

If losses cannot be re-integrated in an appropriate manner, as is generally the case with ruined structures where the potential unity of the monument has been lost because of either lack of factual evidence or extensive damage, the principal aim of the treatment should be to maintain the existing state of the ruins. Any reinforcement or consolidation should then be carried out as a minimum intervention to guarantee the stabilization of the resource, without compromising the appreciation of its aesthetic or architectural values. The interpretation of the history of such sites and the aesthetic values of associated monuments should then be developed from available evidence on the site itself; it can be presented through publications, scale models, fragments or some combination, in a site exhibition or museum.

Anastylosis. Where dismembered original elements still exist at the site, anastylosis can be an acceptable treatment if it is based on reliable evidence regarding the exact original location of these elements. This may contribute to making the original design intent and artistic significance of the monument clearer to the observer. It should be kept in mind, however, that disassembled elements that have weathered on the ground are often decayed to the extent that they have lost their delineated form and are not suitable for an anastylosis.

Accurate anastylosis is difficult to achieve, as experience on many important sites will confirm. Such works should therefore be limited in extent; they should also be reversible and fully documented. If taken too far, anastylosis can make an historic site look like a film set and will diminish its cultural value. Reconstruction using new material implies that the result is a new building, and this means that the historical authenticity is lost in this regard. Reconstructions, particularly when extensive, may result in misinterpretation.

---

9   The theory of treatment of losses or *lacunae* in works of art has been developed at the Istituto Centrale del Restauro, Rome. See Mora, Mora and Philippot, 1977, in the bibliography.

10   See Brandi, 1963, in the bibliography; the *Venice Charter* of 1964; and relevant UNESCO Recommendations.

11   *Venice Charter*, Art. 12.

There are, however, cases when renewal is part of a traditional process which in itself has acquired special significance. This is the case with the periodical redecoration or even reconstruction of Japanese Shinto temples. Such ceremonial renewal should be understood to be outside the modern restoration concept. While the aim of conservation is the *mise-en-valeur* of historic monuments, ensembles or sites as part of modern society without losing their significance or meaning, this does not mean going against living cultural traditions, if these have been maintained in their authenticity as part of society.

Concerning historic areas of special significance (and in particular World Heritage towns), priorities need to be clearly established in order to guarantee the protection and conservation of the entire fabric and infrastructure of the area. Any changes and eventual new constructions that need to be carried out as part of rehabilitation processes should make clear reference to the historical and architectural continuity of the areas concerned.

8.2.4   Treatments related to authenticity in setting

Conservation of cultural heritage, particularly when dealing with larger urban or rural areas, is now recognized as resting within the general field of environmental and cultural development. Sustainable management strategies for change which respect cultural heritage require the integration of conservation attitudes with contemporary economic and social goals, including tourism.

The particular values and characteristics of historic towns and traditional rural settlements should therefore be seen in the larger context of regional or national development planning. This is often the only way to guarantee that their specific functional, social and economic requirements are taken into due consideration in the crucial phases of relevant planning procedures. Authenticity in setting is reflected in the relationship between the resource and its physical context. This includes landscape and townscape values, and also the relationship of man-made constructions to their environmental context.

The preservation of a monument *in situ* is a basic requirement in preserving these values. Treatment of a site will affect the overall setting and values that have been formed and evolved through the historical process. A **ruined monument** has usually acquired specific cultural values and has become part of its setting in the ruined form. This is especially true when the ruin has gained special significance as part of a later creation, such as the ruined mediaeval Fountains Abbey in the setting of the eighteenth-century **landscape garden,** Studley Royal. Similarly, the remains of ancient monuments of Greek or Roman antiquity, recognized as part of our culture in their ruined form, require a strict policy of conservation as ruins. The decision to proceed with an anastylosis should always be related to the historico-physical context of the site and to the overall balance of its setting.

Landscapes are an important issue in themselves. Such is the Lake District in England, which has attracted attention from poets and artists over the centuries. Parallel to this is the Japanese concept of **borrowed landscape** which extends the visual values of a garden beyond its boundaries – a concept much used in Europe from the seventeenth century – and the **cultural landscape** which has matured as a testimony of harmonious interaction between nature and human interventions over a long period. As the cultural landscape is often the product of, and intimately associated with, a particular way of life, any change to that way of life will imply change to the landscape. Can one conserve a complete way of life? It is better for the conservator to think in terms of conserving significant products of that way of life rather than the way of life itself.

Cultural landscape is thus formed of all the environment that has been formed or built by man. Within this some areas may be classified as having special historic interest, i.e., "historic ethnographic, historic associative, or historic adjoining landscapes," or as having "contemporary interest" (P. Goodchild, IoAAS, *pers. comm.*, 1990). All these require due attention, appropriate documentation and planning protection.[12]

Encroachment and intrusive commercial development are typical threats that must be addressed by those responsible for conservation management. In addition, well-intentioned reuse and introduction of new services and infrastructures may detract from the original monuments and their contextually significant setting. Any reception, information areas, and exhibition facilities need to be carefully planned so as to guarantee the integrity of the site. **Buffer zones of sufficient size should be established in order to protect the landscape or historic town context from intrusive elements that diminish cultural values. Planning at local and regional level should take into account the *genius loci* and the enhanced status of a World Heritage site, and ensure that negative threats of all types are prevented or strictly controlled.**

8.3   CONCLUSION

World Heritage is a fragile and **non-renewable, irreplaceable resource.** The aim of safeguarding World Heritage sites is to maintain their **authenticity** and the values for which they have been listed. Therefore, any treatment should be based on the strategy of minimum intervention, and incorporate a programme of routine and preventive maintenance. The degree of intervention and the techniques applied depend upon both the individual resource and the environmental context and climatic conditions to which it is exposed.

The process of resource evaluation will serve as a framework for assigning priorities to representative values, defining management objectives and preparing

---

12   Guidelines for the treatment of historic landscapes are being developed by the US National Parks Service.

presentation strategies. The documents that describe the values and features of a World Heritage site should make the **values** and the **significance** of the resource clear to the general public.

The successful conservation treatment of World Heritage sites depends on an effective evaluation process. Treatments vary according to the character of the monument or site, but should always be based on a **critical judgement**. The consideration of the particular values for which a World Heritage site has been included on the List is of the utmost importance when planning any treatment. Consequently, treatment priorities should be established in accordance with international recommendations, and appropriate action plans should be prepared for the future.

Proposals for major restoration or anastylosis of any site, as well as management proposals that affect the setting, should be submitted to the World Heritage Committee for consideration and comments before any work has been committed. A fundamental strategy to ensure the principle of **minimum intervention** is one that is based on **regular inspections** and **preventive maintenance**.

8.3.1   Checklist for management

✓ Have the fundamental underlying values of your World Heritage resource been **defined** sufficiently?

✓ Have the values been clearly **described** in a document, which has been made **available** to the inhabitants and users of the heritage site?

✓ Do the **inhabitants and users** have adequate appreciation of the values of their heritage?

✓ Are the **objectives of World Heritage conservation** being promoted by existing policies?

✓ Are the **principles** enunciated in international conventions and charters being applied?

✓ Have the **priorities** for conservation treatment been established in relation to values?

✓ In cases where adaptive use is proposed, is historic **authenticity** adequately preserved?

9.1   INTRODUCTION

The period after the Second World War has seen an escalation in industrial development involving the entire globe, as well as a population explosion and excessive consumption of the world's resources. As a result, there has been growing concern for environmentally sustainable development and appropriate resource management, as expressed in international conferences such as those of Stockholm in 1972, the Habitat Conference in Vancouver in 1976, the Rio de Janeiro Conference on the environment in 1992, and the Habitat II Conference in Istanbul in 1996, as well as in the Brundtland Report of the United Nations World Commission on Environment and Development, published in 1987.

The World Heritage Convention reflects this evolution by drawing attention to the universal value of historic settlements and cultural landscapes, where heritage conservation is placed in direct confrontation with values and practical management issues related to economics and community development. Control of change and planning of the built environment tend towards a dynamic process with the purpose of satisfying emerging needs. In addition to safeguarding physical structures and environmental relationships, urban conservation also needs to encompass the maintenance of appropriate functions and, where feasible, traditional types of use. Conservation of historic towns and cultural landscapes necessarily requires the involvement of many different professionals, including city planners, architects, sociologists and administrators. At the same time, an essential part of the work is raising the awareness of the local populace, technicians and administrations about heritage values and the significance of historic structures, advising in the use of traditional materials, regular maintenance and timely repair, as well as establishing criteria for the introduction of new structures and facilities, if unavoidable. Considering the complexity of the task, the scope of these Guidelines is necessarily limited to highlighting some selected aspects of the conservation planning process.

9.1.1   Qualities of historic towns

A well-maintained historic urban centre has many advantages for its citizens. It is intimate and human in scale and often rich in diverse activities; compared with some recently planned cities, it can be extremely convenient for residential use, special public functions, appropriately scaled services, shopping and entertainment. Usually the city is centred around key buildings, such as a cathedral or mosque, a castle or town hall with a market square. For the pedestrian, there are many subtle qualities in streets, lanes, even canals and bridges, and these urban spaces combine to give visual drama by the sensations of compression, expansion, surprise and the careful location of fine architectural set pieces. Views of the principal buildings from various places provide reassuring reference points. Citizens who know the history of the place will enjoy the rich feeling of participating in its history, and a sense of continuity and identity. Some of the key buildings are symbolic; without them, the place would never be the same.

In an historic town, the substance and archaeological potential that embody historic values and material authenticity lie in the structures of all buildings and in the infrastructures. Often a large part of urban fabric may consist of simple buildings without special artistic qualities, anonymous vernacular architecture connected by open squares, lanes, streets, and parks. It is these structures and urban spaces in which the life of the town has evolved that distinguish the concept of historic town from a group of monuments. Since their demolition or neglect would deprive the town of its essence, a policy for their treatment should be established.

❑ *The value of an historic town is embodied in the material testimony of its stones and its structures, and often lies beneath their visible surface. This historical stratigraphy – the evidence and marks brought by changes in use over time, as well as the connections and continuity that make an individual building part of the urban context – constitutes the basis for establishing the criteria for its conservation.*

In Rome, it is possible to see remains of ancient Roman structures in otherwise ordinary-looking structures. Historic cities in the Middle East and North Africa, on the other hand, demonstrate how individual buildings form the continuity of an urban pattern which is made up of residential quarters with services and public areas, and principal commercial areas with facilities such as souks or bazaars. The urban fabric of towns that have been built over a long period of time consists of elements and functions that are closely linked and intermingled.

Authenticity in design is expressed by a number of different aspects in an historic town. This expression is found in the design of the overall town plan, as well as the architectural, artistic, engineering and functional design of individual buildings, and their relationship to each other and to their setting.

❑ *The harmony created by traditional building materials and methods of construction is part of this authenticity, and should be respected.*

Traditional colours based on natural pigments or lime paints should continue to be used. In addition, the texture and scale of the city must be respected and new intrusions avoided. It is the *genius loci* or character of a place that makes it unique and gives it specific quality.

❏ *An historic town is a multi-functional organism with residential, social, political and economic activities. Since this is the essence of an urban organism, the historic area should be properly defined, and these aspects adequately considered and administered.*

In an historic urban area, maintenance and preservation of all buildings and their social functions are fundamental to the town's continuity as an urban entity. In order to prevent structural and economic decay, the conservation plan should include regular inspections by conservation architects. This plan should also consider that historic towns are part of a larger setting, the environment that surrounds them; the only way to ensure proper safeguarding is to extend policies to include the larger planning context.

9.1.2   Threats to historic towns

Today, the traditional and functional whole of historic towns is often threatened, especially in developing countries. Among the numerous causes of decay are:

- demographic growth and the worldwide drift of population from rural areas towards urban centres, leading to social changes and dilapidation in the historic centre, where palaces become commercialized and dwellings often overcrowded and unhealthy;
- increasing use of private motor transport with penetration of areas never meant to be used by such vehicles, which generate atmospheric pollution and destructive vibration;
- development of high-rise buildings, which suffocate historic urban centres by changing their microclimate;
- changes in the methods and scale of industrial and commercial operations, which affect the economic functions of historic areas;
- the drift from craft production to mass production, which demands larger buildings and consequent accumulation of traffic that historic areas cannot accommodate;
- introduction of modern functions and services to replace traditional infrastructures, causing redundancy; and
- lack of maintenance of old buildings and a failure to understand their cultural and functional values, increasing the dangers of decay and collapse.

Modern planners have often failed to understand the cultural value of historic centres, and the unquestioning acceptance of motor traffic has in many instances led to the creation of wide, straight streets through sensitive historic centres, destroying their human scale, the refined traditional structure of their urban fabric, and their narrow winding streets, as well as the relationship between their public and private spaces. The insensitive insertion of modern buildings lacking both cultural roots and good environmental performance is equally damaging to historic centres.

Declining historic areas can be made into attractive livable *foci* for all social categories by reinstating a mixture of residential, commercial, small-scale industrial and leisure activities. Urban management should aim to create harmony, avoid undesirable uses and maintain the existing scale of buildings, as well as their functional and cultural values. The methodology of this approach is called *integrated conservation*.

9.2   OBJECTIVES OF PLANNING

In all town-planning studies affecting historic centres, it is essential to clarify objectives before developing solutions. There are no universal models, as techniques depend upon professional resources and on the social and physical policies that apply to each historic centre.

❑   *In World Heritage towns, the preservation of the fabric by beneficial use is the prime objective.*

On an urban scale, conservation involves not only cultural and historic values but also their inherent economic and social implications. The historic town or city raises conservation problems stemming from the political and economic approach rather than from any physical aspect. The town is the product of several historical periods and of specific social, cultural, anthropological, geographical and economic relationships.

❑   *The historic centre is a constituent of a larger whole and should be studied as part of the present-day dynamic reality, not as a static object of contemplation and tourist attraction.*

Historically, the wealth generated in a town was invested in buildings for worship, monuments, mansions, gardens, etc. Today, the problem is wise control of the continuing wealth that can be generated in a town where private uses at times have to be changed to collective ones. Actions to promote conservation are therefore related to dynamic political instruments rather than statistical or technical means. Thus, the programming of the social and economic use of the town and its region is of the utmost importance.

9.2.1   Integrated conservation

❑   *Integrated conservation implies reconciling conservation requirements and town planning objectives, i.e., considering the values and interests of the existing historic fabric as equal in status to other factors in the general planning process.*

Considering that World Heritage towns are recognized for their "outstanding universal value," it is crucial to guarantee that their authenticity and cultural values are appropriately preserved. Integrated conservation involves the conservation and rehabilitation of historic buildings and areas and the provision of appropriate public services that respect the criteria according to which these areas have been built. In order to be successful in the long term, this process should generally be carried out in collaboration with inhabitants, using planning legislation and norms as a tool.

❏ *The basis for any planning and intervention in an existing fabric is the knowledge and understanding of the resource concerned, in terms of both its history and its present condition.*

❏ *The starting point for conservation planning must be the identification, based on careful study and analysis, of the historic fabric of the town.*

Recent constructions can be understood on the basis of the norms and standards according to which they have been built. The older fabric is generally not understood as well and therefore needs to be carefully studied in order to identify the criteria and technology of its construction. This reading of the fabric is best done through a systematic analysis of the architectural, structural and functional typology of these buildings and their respective urban areas. It should be the basis for conservation planning, which aims to optimize the use of the potential of the historic areas.

❏ *Identification of the historic urban fabric and of modern transformations is facilitated by a comparative study of present cadastral plans and corresponding documents dating from earlier historical periods.*

Different historical periods have had differing laws and customs according to specific technical, social, political or economic motives. Identification of these reasons and the methods of their application (e.g., by study of contemporary manuals) will help to understand the logic behind the construction and positioning of buildings, as well as in the design of public spaces.

Consequently, it is possible to identify the presently existing historic structures and spaces, as well as demolitions and modern additions. These analyses will assist in the physical definition of the existing significant historic areas and eventual buffer zones, and in the preparation of planning norms for their appropriate conservation.

The study of the forces driving growth in the economy of urban areas as a whole could help to ensure the self-preservation of historic areas. It is up to the planners to control development by preventing large intrusive buildings, undesirable traffic flows and out-of-scale functions from disrupting the balance of the city. Tall office blocks should be sited away from the historic centre; even water towers, industrial buildings, and some services can be disruptive if not carefully sited.

❏ *Transportation requirements must be carefully analysed on the basis of the capacity of historic areas to absorb motor vehicles or pedestrian traffic.*

Some historic areas are designed in a manner that makes them form a natural barrier to motor traffic (e.g., streets that are narrow or stepped). In any case, the demands of motor traffic will need to be met according to the essential needs of specific areas. Large vehicles should be prohibited since they harass occupants and accelerate the decay of historic buildings. While guaranteeing internal transportation, motor traffic is best diverted by bypass or ring roads with access spurs into appropriate areas in the historic town.

The UNESCO proposal for conservation of the Old City of Aleppo (Bianca *et al.*, 1980) recognizes all these threats, and provides a basic plan and recommendations for further studies. One of the most significant remarks is repeated here:

> Fundamental structural features of the Islamic fabric such as the introverted layout of its architecture, the integration of single buildings into larger clusters, the coherence of the urban texture and the special character of the pedestrian network were not taken into account [in previous plans]. The specific constraints of the old town in terms of scale and architectural typology allow for only a limited amount of activities directly related to vehicular traffic.

Many historic areas, including even World Heritage towns, are run-down, consisting of almost derelict areas and housing with no proper infrastructure; their traffic problems demonstrate the conflict between the needs of pedestrians and motor vehicles. Due to their long history, they often have complicated patterns of divided ownership. There may also be economic problems, and if the values of their site exceed the value of their building fabric, they are threatened by redevelopment. The integrated conservation of such centres implies joining all political and technical forces and bringing together the skills of the archaeologist, ethnographer, sociologist and historian with those of the architect and engineer in an interdisciplinary collaboration, under the leadership of a conservation-conscious, qualified town planner.

9.2.2   Control of change

❑ *One of the objects of urban conservation is to control the rate of change in the urban system. We therefore need to comprehend the life forces of that system and the potential causes of its decay.*

The urban fabric tends to last a long time because of the relative durability of construction materials. By contrast, the human activities which have to be accommodated within the fabric change more rapidly (living standards, sizes of families, modes of production, changes introduced by technology such as the motor car and television, dislocation through war or natural disaster). With time, there is a possibility for conflicts associated with real or apparent obsolescence of buildings and infrastructures. If appropriate precautions are not taken, this may lead to a planning blight that will further degrade the existing structures.

There are two major types of obsolescence:

- physical-*cum*-structural or functional, and
- locational or environmental, caused by noise, traffic or air pollution.

Planning blight is an economic disease caused by lack of decision or overly ambitious failed attempts to speed up modernization. It can also be caused by failure to provide a disaster plan in seismic or flood-prone zones. On the basis of a well-prepared typological-functional analysis and of a rehabilitation programme, urban conservation management should be able to absorb these changes, relieve the conflict and promote a gradual improvement in derelict areas. Besides, experience demonstrates that **minimum interventions at key points in time are best for the community.**

The urban and regional systems of cities, towns and villages have evolved over the centuries under the stimulus of forces within which private or public sector entrepreneurs and landowners can make decisions. In most communities this action has been controlled by governmental or local conditions which have imposed some constraints. In the past, the use of consistent building technology and style created harmony, and the scale of operations was limited. Only in the twentieth century has urban and regional planning been introduced as a means of dealing with the conflict between unrestrained, self-interested market forces and community goals and objectives.

Such planning has become a governmental function with its own laws, administrative machinery and financial adjustments. The function typically embraces plan preparation, plan implementation, and plan review. The generic process obviously varies from country to country and from time to time; it should relate to the culture and customs of each individual country and to the professional resources available within that country. It is a mistake to borrow ready-made systems, as they may not correspond to the needs or wishes of the people themselves. World Heritage towns should be places in which people dwell, pursue their work, and enjoy their leisure time; they are not museums.

9.3   PLANNING PROCEDURE

While being aware of the difference between general physical planning and planning in areas distinguished by specific cultural values, one can identify a model for a town planning process which has been adopted throughout the world with varying degrees of emphasis and adaptation. The process involves:

- identification of the current situation;
- some prediction of future events without the planning intervention;
- formulation of optional future possibilities which would arise with the planning intervention;
- assessment of such options for feasibility and desirability;
- detailing of the options selected;
- formulation of a programme for implementation of the options with the necessary means – legal, administrative, financial, etc.; and

- review of such options, in the light of experience, following implementation; this requires monitoring of events on a regular basis.

A typical master town plan for an urban area has two basic components. The first consists of the current and future profile of the users of the plan area (that is, those resident in or making use of it in their everyday activities). The second component is providing them with the appropriate mix of land uses for those activities, such as industry, shopping centres and schools, so that appropriate physical development will occur.

In the case of historic cities and towns of World Heritage status, the normal urban planning techniques – such as studies of demographic trends, population movements, traffic and transport (including growth in motor-car ownership), and proposals for zoning of activities and allocation of space for new development and improved traffic circulation – are often too rigid and generally inadequate.

The concept of zoning – the limiting of an area to a specific category of use – is contrary to the cultural richness and social diversity of a thriving historic centre. Statistics based on zoning will not provide sufficiently accurate information on specific properties. There is also a risk in the application of standards without due consideration of the existing historic reality, which could result in the destruction of the existing scale and urban texture.

The social problems in historic areas will require full study using methodologies appropriate to the local conditions. The pattern of ownership and effect of the State Party's traditions and legal practices requires careful consideration. If these or their inconsiderate application work against effective management, changes may have to be introduced gradually or by legislation. Education and training are significant factors in this matter.

National and provincial plans can have a fundamental impact on World Heritage sites. Such plans should be studied carefully and any amendments thought necessary for conservation management should be suggested in time. Typical threats include plans for new roads, the siting of industries and the emission of polluting gases. Conservation of a World Heritage site must be given a high priority at all levels of town planning, from the communal master plan to district, provincial and national strategies.

❑ *In many ways the problems encountered in World Heritage towns are related to more general environmental issues and control of development.*

These issues were clearly expressed in the report of the World Commission on Environment and Development in 1987 (United Nations, 1987), and in the Tokyo Declaration of the same year and published in that same report. While these reports recognize poverty as a major source of environmental degradation, they stress the need for international collaboration to change the quality of growth and to conserve and enhance the resource base. This will mean reorienting technology and managing risk factors, as well as integrating environmental concerns and economics into the decision-making process. In terms of cultural heritage, this new approach will strengthen the demand for **integrated conservation planning,** with realistic management and **sustainable development** of our existing cultural resources.

National and local authorities often have conflicting views about town planning priorities. These can only be resolved by starting from the existing situation and using a systematic inspection approach to identify the exact state and condition of the resource.

9.3.1 Inspections and surveys

❑ *The town plan should relate to the potential in the existing building fabric. Detailed inspection of all surviving historic fabric will give planners a chance to plan realistically, using cultural resources to the best advantage.*

The management of historic urban areas is distinguished from conventional urban planning by the fact that inspections are carried out at regular intervals. If one knows exactly what is there and has a full record, archaeological values can be identified; sometimes buildings that appear unprepossessing conceal important structures that are worthy of restoration.

There are many ways in which regular inspections can be arranged. If local professional skills are inadequate, a panel of suitable architects can be approved by the Site Commission, and guidelines on procedure prepared. Depending on circumstances, it would benefit the site if the Commission were to subsidize or meet the full cost of this work. Property owners would have to be prepared to give access, but should do this readily if they receive copies of the report on their property and come to realize that regular inspections reduce the long-term cost of caring for property.

9.3.2 Implementation

In many countries, planning procedures work downwards from country to province, region to towns; the same may be true in cases where the primary responsibility has been given to individual communes. The authority responsible for implementation will steer, influence or control the actions of both development and conservation and renewal agencies. The plan-making authority may also have distinct implementation functions for particular sectors, such as the provision of infrastructure elements such as water supply, drainage and sewage, electricity, roads, parking spaces and housing, as well as conservation of historic buildings and historic centres. Implementation will necessarily be an ongoing activity, starting during the town planning process; likewise there will be periodic monitoring and review of the plan.

❑ *The conservation planner tends to work upwards, assessing the values of an object, site or historic centre; first documenting its history and present condition, then proposing the minimum intervention needed to prevent decay.*

❑ *Decay can have economic and cultural causes as well as physical causes. Conservation can only delay deterioration from physical causes but, by encouraging public awareness of the value of the site, it can change cultural attitudes and, with the help of planning, remove the economic causes of decay.*

Conservation planning is especially important with regard to rehabilitation in historic centres. However, even countries with sophisticated town planning programmes in place often do not take into account the actual condition of the cultural heritage and its capacity for alternative uses. (Rehabilitation is an economic necessity in most historic areas, and will be discussed later.)

❑ *The planner should respect not only historic buildings and spaces, but also the intangible elements of cultural heritage expressed as community values or folk life. The aim of planning should be to see that the planned change avoids, as far as is practicable, disruption of traditional and contemporary community patterns. While it is not feasible to freeze folk life in time, it is desirable to facilitate change by respecting the choices of the people concerned.*

9.3.3   Demands on staff

The planning process, when properly carried out with all the necessary studies, makes heavy demands on professional staff. Not every country has sufficient staff to organize a sophisticated planning system that respects the needs of the people. Indeed, town planning tends to be so complicated that the layman often gives up trying to understand the procedures and the logic behind them; long delays in decision-making do not help this matter.

One of the objectives in conservation planning should be to establish a system of communication with property owners and to provide them with guidelines for the treatment of their properties. The possibility may be extended by the designation of conservation areas and the nomination of an architect-planner, together with an assessor, to administer the guidelines. This method, though not perfect, will provide a quick way for initiating the necessary protection of sites in developing countries.

9.3.4   Conservation report and plan

The next step in the conservation planning procedure is the preparation, by independent consultants, of a conservation report on an historic centre. This report would include both archive research and a series of physical surveys. The results should be brought together and illustrated using maps of appropriate scales.[1] The conservation plan and the norms for implementation will be based on this report, with due regard for the applicable rules and regulations, and should be duly worked out in consultation with property owners. A series of practical guidelines or manuals will be useful to provide property owners with information on technical questions.

The report and the plan would consist of surveys and documents, namely:

- **Maps**: the basic maps showing the town as a whole and the historic centre in particular.
- **Ownership**: maps showing ownership and present use of historic properties.
- **History**: illustration of the general historical development of the overall urban area, with particular attention to core areas. A survey showing the ages and historical phases of the existing building stock should be prepared.
- **Typology**: (a) surveys of the architectural, structural and functional typology of buildings; (b) the typology of public and private open spaces; (c) townscape and landscape analyses.
- **Condition**: a survey of the physical condition of individual historic properties, and the infrastructure and services in the respective conservation areas.
- **Conservation Plan:** consisting of a map to define the proposed conservation policy and the degrees of treatment, as well as of the norms and regulations for implementation.

Maps and Ownership: A series of maps are needed as a basis for work, showing the whole town and the historic areas to a scale that allows individual properties and their boundaries to be identified (i.e., 1:500 or 1:1 250). A map is required that shows ownership and users of properties (i.e., private, social, commercial, industrial, religious, etc.), and such a map could effectively combine land registry information and cadastral survey data through cooperation with the local authorities. It is useful to compare present ownership with a previous stage in order to identify the impact of modern development. In a more advanced stage, it may be desirable to prepare maps showing the floor plans of the fabric. The survey should also provide information on infrastructure and geological conditions in the area.

History: A series of maps should be prepared to illustrate the historical development of the overall urban area with particular attention to core areas. The causes of development or decline in different periods should be identified. This survey should be accompanied by a complete bibliographical study and a collection of historic drawings, engravings, maps and earlier town plans. It is important, as part of the analysis, to verify the extent to which town plans have been implemented, and which elements in the present urban fabric relate to each phase. This survey is essential for establishing not only the criteria for the construction of

---

1   The maps could use either colours or hatchings to identify different types of information, but hatchings are to be preferred as they allow easy reproduction of black-and-white working copies by photocopying.

existing physical structures, but also for identifying their functional areas as a basis for eventual rehabilitation. The ages and historical phases of buildings should be identified, and a map should show buildings and areas that are under special protection by the authorities.[2]

Typology and Condition: Surveys and the resulting analytical maps will indicate the typology of historic buildings, and of public and private open spaces. These are based on a recording and survey of historic buildings aiming at a clarification of the criteria for their design and construction. Different building elements should be recorded and referenced to contemporary manuals when possible in relation to their function, materials, and methods of construction (e.g., layout, floor structure, roofs, courts, position of staircases, doors, windows). Properties can be categorized according to their type and function (e.g., public buildings, community or religious complexes, palaces, residential row houses, courtyard houses, etc.).

This analysis should be accompanied by documented information, including:

- a survey of the transformations over time,
- clarification of the condition of the properties, and
- definition of the social and economic status of respective areas.

These documents form a basic reference for recommendations on treatment. The survey may be extended to a townscape or landscape analysis that takes into account the design criteria and indicates important ensembles, spaces and areas of amenity, historic parks and gardens, views of buildings or streets, and views out of the historic centre, serving as a reference for both conservation planning and eventual modern development in the region. In this context, it is vital that buildings important for the citizens' sense of identity should be indicated.

The Conservation Master Plan is a document summarizing the conclusions resulting from the above analyses. It will consist of a Map of the Master Conservation Plan and the Norms for Implementation. The plan will define the proposed conservation policy in each area concerned, and will indicate the parameters for treatment in particular buildings or areas. Clear indications should be made of areas for special protection, buffer zones, and the areas where guidelines should apply. In addition, the plan should identify areas where large buildings should not be erected, as well as the zones and the conditions for modern development (i.e., large or tall buildings, industrial sites, etc.) that will avoid damaging values in the historically valuable areas. This document should be the fundamental reference for integrated conservation planning for both the city as a whole and the individual properties that belong to it.

---

2   The criteria for listing buildings should be agreed upon, but, at the very least, all buildings over 100 years old should be included, as well as many 80 years old; more recent buildings should be listed when there are special reasons. Listed buildings may be graded (e.g., *Grade 1*: National Interest; *Grade 2*: Provincial or District Interest; *Grade 3*: Local or Townscape Value). Although the grades should affect the management of these properties, they should not be taken as a basis for evaluation since historical values in urban conservation refer to the fabric of the entire city or town.

This question of use should be addressed in the **Conservation Master Plan;** it should be based both on systematic analysis of the typology and conditions of the building stock, and on the needs and requirements (e.g., accessibility, services) of the area. In the case of buildings that have the potential for public or community functions, town planners, estate managers and architects can work together. The town planner should know whether an historic centre area is deficient in any type of facility – e.g., a library or school – and the architect should be aware of suitability of buildings and the surrounding areas for the proposed uses. The estate manager can find the user and arrange legal details of tenure. **By the combination of these skills, but most especially that of the estate or property manager, it is possible to raise an historic centre from dereliction to prosperity.**

9.3.5   Degrees of intervention

For the built environment, the conservation role stems from the existing physical stock of buildings. Where use values predominate, there may have been continuous changes to meet changing socio-economic conditions. Furthermore, in any particular year the relative proportion of development that is carried out is generally small compared with the total existing urban fabric.

From this, it follows that the conservation plan should consider the current stock of buildings as it evolves over its life cycle, as well as the changes planned for the future. Conservation by rehabilitation is a major feature in planning the future of an urban area; the conservation option must always take priority over the development option.

9.3.6   Maintenance

❑ *Regular maintenance is necessary to preserve the fabric of buildings.*

Buildings made of earth need annual attention to roofs and walls; in Africa, lime plaster on walls needs renewal every 2-3 years. Metals need protection from corrosion, wood from insects and fungal attack; in humid climates, repainting is essential maintenance. In many countries, it is considered good practice to keep the paint work of all houses with their outbuildings in good condition and renew it regularly. This creates an environment which is typical and expressive of local attitudes; such traditions may have gone out of practice in some countries due to rapid socio-economic changes interrupting maintenance traditions, or the architecture may consist of more durable building materials that have led to a different approach to patinated surfaces (such as in Italy).

Any repainting should be done with due respect for the original colour scheme and type of paint, as based on historical study supported by technical research. In Nikko, Japan, there is a temple that is re-lacquered every 25 years while a nearby seventeenth-century tomb has all its original decoration in slightly faded condition; both are appropriate in their context, as tradition has established certain procedures that are compatible with the function of the building. Nowadays, traditional pigments and paint vehicles are difficult to obtain. Lead has been banned as a paint component in most countries and present-day pigments are ground much finer. Contemporary paints designed for concrete or similar surfaces are often unsuitable for historic buildings as they do not breathe; they form an impermeable vapour barrier that can be destructive when it traps moisture. Not only do these paints fail to age gracefully, but they are also difficult to repaint. It is recommended that the management of a World Cultural Heritage Site lay down a policy for painting and redecoration. There may be a need to revert to traditional techniques and prepare paints using traditional recipes. If necessary, special dispensation may have to be obtained for specific use of materials otherwise excluded from normal trade, as has occurred in the United Kingdom with regard to Grade I listed buildings.

9.3.7   Rehabilitation

In the urban planning context, **revitalization** means the planning measures that are necessary to improve the social and economic activities of an historic area or an historic town, which has lost its original functional vitality and, as a consequence, historic buildings and urban spaces have become redundant and dilapidated. The aim of revitalization should be an appropriate balance between conservation and development.

The revitalization of an historic area which is economically run-down may require the rehabilitation of a large number of typical dwellings, as well as of obsolete buildings such as redundant churches, convents, warehouses and factories.

Rehabilitation means the physical improvements that are necessary in order to provide an appropriate use to an empty or inappropriately utilized structure. Rehabilitation should always involve a use as close as possible to the original function so as to ensure a minimum intervention and minimum loss of cultural values; this also makes sense economically.

❑   *The closer the new use of the rehabilitated building is to its original use, the less the work will cost and the better it is for the urban plan as a whole.*

Often superficial blemishes and lack of maintenance persuade people that buildings should be pulled down. However, if the foundations, walls and floors are in reasonable condition, a house can generally be rehabilitated, even if this means giving it a new roof together with all the amenities of modern hot and cold water and electrical and mechanical services.

❑   *While the partial rebuilding of a single structure that has been seriously damaged (e.g., by an earthquake or neglect) may be done responsibly, attention needs to be paid to the quality of such treatment and its impact on the scale of the historic town fabric as a whole.*

In such cases, any substantial parts of the building, such as standing walls, should, if possible, be maintained *in situ*, and new construction should be carried out in compatible materials and using appropriate technology. It has been observed that a coherent structure is safer and more resistant (e.g., to seismic action) than a mixed structural system consisting of a combination of traditional stone and timber with modern steel and concrete. Any proposals for structural consolidation should be preceded by a thorough evaluation of the existing structural system, so that it can be used to its maximum potential.

❑ *If additions are required, they should be built in materials that are compatible with those of the existing structure. If traditional materials are not available, new materials should be utilized in a manner that does not undermine the conservation of the original structure.*

Insertion of structurally determinate (rigid) contemporary frame structures within an existing indeterminate system may have an adverse effect due to their additional weight and their differing response to seismic action. Another consideration is that excessive use of new materials could change a traditional urban fabric to the point where its authenticity is compromised.

Conservation should not restrict the living standards of the occupants of an historic area. However, there is a challenge implicit in meeting the rising expectations of present-day life-styles. If the occupants are to have cars, for example, provision must be made for parking that does not interfere with the existing fabric. In addition, needs for water, electricity, and possibly gas should be met, and sewage and rainwater disposal should be dealt with. Consideration must also be given to acoustic privacy; sources of noise – especially restaurants and clubs – must be contained.

❑ *New services should not be introduced into an historic area without a clear understanding of its ability to absorb, use and maintain them. Present-day standards may not be compatible with the inhabitants' way of life or the existing infrastructure (e.g., availability of water, electricity, means of waste disposal).*

Specific guidelines for the **rehabilitation** of an historic area should be worked out according to its local cultural and physical conditions. Examples can be found in the Standards and Guidelines adopted by the United States Department of the Interior (Anon. 1983), or in the guidelines prepared for the master plan of Lamu in Kenya (Siravo and Pulver, 1986). Such guidelines should comply with international recommendations and, in the case of World Heritage sites, with the requirements of the Convention.

9.3.8 Infill design

❑ *It is the primary objective of conservation planning, particularly concerning World Heritage sites, to give strict priority to the conservation of existing historic fabric. The building of new structures should not be an excuse for demolishing old ones. New construction may, however, be necessary to re-establish functional and architectural continuity, and in cases where empty lots might be hazardous to or further decay surrounding buildings.*

Infill buildings are by definition contemporary constructions, and should therefore express the spirit of the day; at the same time, their design should also take into consideration the design of their historic context. The design of infill buildings should be based on a clear and systematic analysis of the historical morphology of the existing urban fabric and its functions. In principle, it should aim to re-integrate the lacunae in the urban fabric. Solutions to the design problem will vary according to the specific cultural values and traditions of the historic area, the type and condition of the existing structures, the degree of homogeneity of the place, etc.

While it is impossible to provide precise general guidelines that apply to all infill structures in all historic areas, specific guidelines can be established for particular cultural regions or sites. The following points may be useful in highlighting some aspects for consideration. The new building should have:

- a **rhythm** that harmonizes with the urban rhythms and the morphological pattern of the surrounding fabric;
- a **mass** in balance in its context – not too large to spoil the intimate human scale of the historic centre, and not based on an artificial combination of several lots to accommodate one large function;
- a **street** boundary line following the line of the existing setbacks;
- a **silhouette** respecting the traditional local character and silhouette;
- **materials** that are traditional, or compatible with traditional materials;
- **windows** similar in character and in window:wall ratio to typical buildings in the same area; and be of
- **high quality** in construction and design, which might be achieved by careful proportions and – in appropriate cases – by elevational relief or plastic treatment.

Factors related to townscape rarely justify the reproduction of a lost building; such a solution is generally considered architectural pastiche. The practice of facadism (i.e., retaining the facade and building a new construction behind) undermines the basic principles of urban conservation, as it results from the demolition of existing fabric, and is generally accompanied by the introduction of new, otherwise incompatible, large-scale functions into the historic fabric. New construction in historic centres should be restricted to filling in gaps in the urban fabric; infill structures should possess artistic vitality and be designed according to the highest standards, in harmony with the scale and character of the World Heritage site into which they are inserted.

9.3.9 Administrative actions

The urban system is a complex collection of diverse resources which are interdependent and should be regarded as a whole. The simplest level comprises the urban services and facilities: water supply, sewerage, electricity, traffic and parking. Some resources are exhaustible but renewable (e.g., vegetation), but historic buildings do not come into this category. Private management of non-renewable resources with a get-rich-quick objective can exhaust such resources quickly. The successful management of World Heritage sites depends on broader aims. The return need not be financial, but can be in terms of social benefit, status, prestige or politics.

The administrators of World Heritage towns have to face the present realities, which exercise considerable pressures on historic centres. In most societies today, the traditional way of life is changing, and this produces, amongst other things, profound and rapid mutations in the character of towns, where the population is concentrated and contemporary culture seeks expression. Cities are the privileged victims of change and, for this reason, it is increasingly necessary to manage change; this is the challenge that confronts their administrations.

When the control of change has to be exercised within the conservation policy for a World Heritage town, these problems present a higher level of challenge to those who have been elected and appointed to manage them. In order not to be suffocated by their older buildings, and in order not to succumb to the darker aspects of the present, these historic cities should be managed by well-informed, qualified professionals with vision. There should be a multi-disciplinary committee responsible for the conservation of the city's historic fabric, following well-established regulations and using an efficient method to monitor the effect of its actions.

To sum up, the management of historic urban areas involves:

- **analysis of urban morphology**, with systematic studies of building typology, condition, use and occupancy, as well as identification of economic causes of growth and decay;
- **property management**, with **regular inspections**, and a **maintenance strategy**, including control of external painting and decoration;
- **modest rehabilitation schemes**, rather than ambitious ones; and
- **social input** and **consultation with occupants**.

❑ *Conservation Planning is an activity designed to bridge the preferred future to the present; it is a critical element of the management of cultural resources.*

9.4   CHECKLIST FOR URBAN CONSERVATION

The Site Committee will be faced with many specific questions, such as:

- ✓ Have the **fundamental underlying values** of the World Heritage town been defined sufficiently?

- ✓ Are the **objectives** of World Heritage conservation being promoted by existing policies?

- ✓ Are the **principles** enunciated in international conventions and charters being applied?

- ✓ Are the applicable **laws and regulations** up to date?

- ✓ Is their **application** effective? If not, where does it fail?

- ✓ Do the **inhabitants** have adequate perception of the values of their heritage?

- ✓ Is the **infrastructure** adequate and in good order?

- ✓ Is there resistance to conservation policies from **property owners**?

- ✓ How should the inertia and absenteeism of **interested parties** be avoided?

- ✓ How should the **duty of protection** *versus* the financial attraction from redevelopment or rehousing at increased densities be reconciled?

- ✓ Is the **relationship** between property owners and experts satisfactory?

- ✓ Are the procedures for **implementing plans** for conservation working satisfactorily?

- ✓ What is the **cost of interventions** aimed at protection and rehabilitation?

- ✓ Have all **financing** options been explored? Will private foundations and trusts assist? Can revolving funds be applied? Are the difficulties of finance insuperable?

- ✓ Do higher levels of **government** give financial assistance?

- ✓ What proportion of **foreign tourist income** is devoted to conservation?

- ✓ Are there **financial and fiscal incentives** to encourage property owners to maintain or rehabilitate their properties?

- ✓ Are the controls for **financial and fiscal assistance** adequate?

- ✓ Is **rent control** necessary to prevent displacement of sitting tenants?

- ✓ Is it possible to obtain a **reasonable financial return** on rehabilitation if historic authenticity and archaeological values are preserved?

✓ How is **historic authenticity** preserved when adaptive re-use is proposed?

✓ How are **cultural, economic and fiscal impacts** of programmes evaluated?

✓ Is there **proper documentation** of historic quarters and individual buildings?

✓ Are there **regular inspections** of historic buildings?

✓ Are there **subsidies** to encourage owners to commission such inspections and reports?

✓ Is there a **maintenance strategy**?

✓ Are there **craftspeople and materials** available to execute maintenance, repairs and restoration of historic buildings?

✓ Is there sufficient **expertise** available?

- architects
- engineers
- archaeologists
- art historians
- conservators
- administrators

✓ Can **demographic movements** (i.e., overcrowding, or conversely the flight of residence from historic centres) be influenced?

✓ What is the **social impact of tourism** on the residents?

✓ Can **over-utilization of historic centres by tourists** be mitigated and if so, by whom?

✓ What are the **plus values** of a World Heritage town and how are these exploited?

10.1   INTRODUCTION

The tourism industry is now part of our culture and international economy, second only to the oil industry in financial terms. Tourism is dynamic but should not be developed too quickly; rather, it should be allowed to grow provided the capacity of the site and the supporting infrastructure are not exceeded. As stated in the Manila Declaration of the World Tourism Organization, economic gain is not the sole aim of tourism. Tourism should improve the quality of life of the local population without compromising the indigenous culture.

❑ *Visiting a World Heritage site can be an intellectual experience; visitors who are prepared will benefit the most.*

Most visitors to World Heritage sites are seeking an outing, a change of scene, or an experience to relate to the folks back home. Some are interested in their cultural heritage, others in the archaeology or architecture. Part of the manager's task is to make the visit enjoyable and interesting for everyone; this will help to generate political support for conservation, foreign currency, jobs and income. Hopefully, some people will go away more interested in their culture than when they came.

If schoolchildren do not enjoy their visit, they may avoid all World Heritage sites for many years and not introduce their own children to them. They are a difficult group to keep interested, but it is not in the long-term interest of conservation for them to come and then to be disappointed; better for them not to come at all.

Making visits enjoyable and interesting is achieved by thinking about the interests and attitudes of the visitors before thinking of the resources, and this can be difficult for heritage site managers, many of whom consider the visitors only as an afterthought. Experts in tourism, visitor management, presentation and marketing will be of great assistance; surveys of visitors will help to identify their interests, where they come from, how long they are staying, whether they will come back again and how much money they might spend.

The **management plan** for the heritage site should state the visitor service objectives. The objectives will need to be discussed with the Site Commission, local authorities and tourist bodies to ensure that there is no conflict. This plan will have to address such issues as income from entry charges, benefit of local tourist businesses, potential damage to the heritage resource, how to deal with disappointed visitors, congestion, reduction of visitors at peak times and the mix of visitors. Useful distinctions can be made between people on tour, vacationers, day visitors, school parties, conference delegates and visiting experts, and the management plan could have different objectives for each.

10.1.1   Needs of visitors

All visitors appreciate:

- a friendly welcome and help with any problems or accidents;
- a clean, litter-free and well-maintained site;
- guidance on local taboos and religious or cultural attitudes (e.g., towards pigs in Islamic countries, cows in Hindu countries, appropriate attire and behaviour in religious sites, etc.);
- presentation of the story of the monument or site and its treasures in a way they can understand; and
- security and protection for themselves and their possessions.

By international agreement, visitors who spend the night away from home are called tourists. These people will need hotels, hostels, camp sites, restaurants and several types of transport; they may also require shops to meet their specific needs. Providing all of these is important for cultural heritage sites, for without them the culture will be inaccessible to many. Such services are not the normal function of site managers, but they do require cooperation between public authorities and the private sector.

❑ *Good visitor management will reduce the need for expenditure upon promoting and advertising the heritage site: its attractiveness will become known to – and hence publicized by – the mass media. In many cases, there is a conflict of policy between site managers who want visitor numbers restricted so that sites are not damaged, and tourist boards or commercial interests who want to use the sites to attract visitors to the area.*

10.1.2   Vandalism and damage

Vandalism often results from boredom, and, on cultural heritage sites, good presentation will make it less likely. Many other security problems can be resolved by good management, coupled with occasional firm policing. Unfortunately, tourism can cause excessive wear and tear; although there are no well-documented studies of damage by visitors, circumstantial evidence indicates it increases the cost of conservation. In holy places, visitors should be instructed to be quiet and to avoid flash photography. Smoking and litter disposal should be controlled, visitors should keep to paths and be forbidden to pick wild flowers and scrawl graffiti.

10.1.3   Welcoming the visitors

❏ *The attitude of staff towards visitors is the single most important factor in making their visit enjoyable. Each visitor should be welcomed as personally as possible and there should be an obvious and clearly-marked source of help in case of accident or difficulty. Any specific dangers should be pointed out, including dangerous animals or plants, theft, etc.*

Nothing spoils a visitor's experience more than being robbed, especially of a passport, camera or irreplaceable exposed film. Custodial staff, while treating visitors as guests to be welcomed and helped, also have to keep an eye out for theft or damage. It is important for staff to be polite at all times, however annoying the visitor.

Signs and large-scale plans showing the layout of the site should be installed in the parking lots, as well as wherever else strangers could lose their way. Fix signs where they will not cause damage to ancient structures or spoil views. Close observation of visitor behaviour is helpful in strategic placement of signs.

The purpose of signs should be to help the visitor and not necessarily to direct attention to the most important treasures. Guides should wear arm-bands or uniforms so that they can be easily identified and asked for help. Souvenir vendors, beggars and self-styled guides should not be allowed in heritage sites, where they distract and harass visitors. Taxi and rickshaw drivers should also be controlled.

10.2   SITE MAINTENANCE

The best way to discourage litter is immediately to pick up any that is dropped. Litter bins should be emptied regularly. In some countries, less litter is dropped if there are no litter bins at all. In others, fines for littering are a deterrent. Where part of a heritage site is used for entertainment or special events, it is best if the organizers are required to remove all litter, special equipment, stands, etc., as soon as the event is over.

Special uses of the heritage site for making films can be both profitable and bring good publicity. Nevertheless, film makers and television crews need clear instructions to prevent them from inadvertently damaging the resource. The heat generated by their lighting can damage cultural material and is a fire hazard.

Parking lots should be kept clean, and puddles or mud patches should be filled in. Warnings against theft should be erected. Large parking areas near heritage sites should be broken up by mounds, planting and landscaping, or avoided altogether. Where remote parking lots are used, provision should be made to help elderly and handicapped persons to reach the site.

10.3   PRESENTATION AND INTERPRETATION

All World Heritage sites have more than one important story to tell about their history: the way they were constructed or destroyed, the people who lived there, the various activities there and the happenings, the previous uses of the site and perhaps tales of the notable treasures. In presenting and interpreting the historical story of the heritage site, it is necessary to be selective and to decide which elements will be of most interest to the kind of people that the site will attract; human interest stories are often the most popular.

❑   *The aims of the interpretation of the heritage site need to be clearly established before work starts, and reviewed regularly in the light of experience and changing thinking.*

The media used to interpret the history of the site should be chosen to be as effective as possible for all visitors, without harming the appearance or ambience of the heritage site. For instance, the equipment for Sound and Light (*Son et lumière*) performances may harm ancient walls or obstruct the overall setting during daylight hours. Signs explaining things may spoil views or cause damage by their fixings. Media used for interpretation could include:

- clearly written notices, didactic panels, plans, leaflets, guidebooks, souvenir books and reference books in various languages, as required;
- human guides or teachers;
- museums, exhibitions, models, samples of building materials, copies of art objects, pictures or coins;
- dioramas, listening posts, portable tape players; and
- films, television, video, tape/slide shows, plays, music, Sound and Light performances, and lighting to accent features.

Mistakes are easily made in the use of media: money can be wasted; the appearance of the site can be compromised; guided tours can disturb other visitors; and leaflets and didactic panels can be poorly written. It is best to start by determining the message to be conveyed and establishing the audience. Each site is unique, and what has worked on one heritage site may not be effective for all. A substantial budget has to be allowed, and skilled advice sought for the interpretation of all heritage sites of world significance.

It is often useful to sell a simple guidebook which is easily understandable to those with little or no previous knowledge of the site; this could be designed to fill in some of the gaps in historical knowledge. Serious students should have detailed guidebooks that have been checked for accuracy by experts, are free of speculative interpretation and include references for further information.

General tourist information is often provided on heritage sites. This is a useful and sometimes profitable service, ranging from selling tourist guides and maps to giving advice, making reservations at hotels and theatres, providing leaflets about other attractions and advising upon transport. If such a service is extensive, it should be separated from information about the heritage site proper, so that queues do not develop. Well-illustrated souvenir books which remind people of their visit, picture postcards and books on various subjects related to the site can provide an important source of income.

The didactic panels explaining the site will have to be well-designed and made of durable material, with attractive lettering and carefully chosen colours. They should all use the same graphic style, which should be clearly distinguishable from that used for direction or warning signs. Avoid technical language, except in parenthesis. Since they will often be the most important part of the interpretation of the site, their presentation should be given high priority. It is advisable to assign a single, visually-aware person responsibility for the design and siting of all signs; and also control of the quantity of signs on the site.

Audio-visual presentations have to be of the highest quality, and normally about 10-15 minutes is the maximum acceptable length. Sound and Light presentations can be much longer, but care must be taken to ensure that the script is dramatic, historically accurate and without prejudice or discrimination.

Scaled-down or full-sized reproductions can be used to help explain past happenings on the site, and these have the advantage that they can be replaced when they become damaged or wear out. As far as possible, the same, traditional, materials of the original should be used, as modern materials, such as plastics, will not weather in the same way.

Since languages that are widespread (such as English and French) are pronounced differently throughout the world, it cannot be assumed that they will be understood by visitors, even native speakers. This factor can affect the use of listening posts and human guides to the extent that sometimes it is better to use only written material. Display screens that can be interrogated by push button and give a written or diagrammatic answer, provide an alternative to listening posts.

Human guides must be well-trained and knowledgeable, and either licensed by the state or employed by the heritage site management. School parties should be assembled and briefed about the site in an area set aside for the purpose, preferably indoors. Staff instructors can help the children's own teachers explain the heritage site, and it is a help if visiting teachers can be invited to see the site and be briefed in advance of the parties they are bringing. The availability of educational materials for teachers would be useful in this context.

Archaeological digs can be explained by panels or a guide, or both, and special provision for easy viewing, such as visitor observation platforms, may be required in order to avoid interrupting those digging. Information needs to be updated on a regular basis, but special discoveries could be announced to the press only at times when it is not likely to add to visitor-management problems.

Children will understand the story of a heritage site better if they can talk to actors playing historic roles, watch or even take part in re-enactments of great events, listen to ballads, or see Sound and Light performances with live actors. The actors should be present on the right occasions and the performances heavily publicized. The show should suit the specific audience; the information should be accurate, but some artistic licence may be permitted.

10.4   VISITOR MANAGEMENT

Techniques of visitor management can ensure that the sheer number of visitors does not detract from general enjoyment of the site, prevent a proper appreciation of it or cause physical harm to historic resources. These techniques can also reduce maintenance costs and increase income.

Excessive visitor pressure can be reduced if there are other attractions nearby. These might include a zoo, aquarium, leisure park, beach or live entertainment. Since the most vulnerable heritage sites are those which are well-known and promoted, with no other attractions in the vicinity, tourist boards could be discouraged from over-publicizing vulnerable heritage sites. They can also help develop counter-attractions or divert attention to lesser-known heritage sites with spare capacity.

❑ *Peak loadings can be reduced if there is a booking system for coach parties and a limit to the number of visitors admitted at any one time.*

❑ *Small changes in the times of arrival can greatly ease the pressures.*

❑ *It is useful to have alternative routes for visiting parties so that if several arrive at once they can be separated, or taken on routes of different lengths.*

Wear on floors can be reduced by putting down strip coverings of carpet, canvas, rubber, etc. Grass can be maintained by regularly moving footpaths a meter or so to one side. It is not so easy to repair the damage resulting from the touch of thousands of hands, or from human breath, and controls to keep people at a safe distance may be necessary in some cases.

Visitors should be allowed to view heritage sites at their own speed. Where, for security reasons or lack of space, individual viewing is not possible, the speed of circulation of guided parties can be varied and visitors given a choice between quick tours and slower, more detailed ones. As crowds inside buildings can raise the relative humidity to damaging levels, the number of visitors at any one time may need to be strictly controlled.

❑ *Visitor routes should allow for the natural tendency of people to turn left on entering any space.*

❑ *Shops should be conveniently located near the entrance and exit of the site.*

Entry charges need to be determined such that services for visitors can be improved without reducing the funds available for conservation work, which must be kept separate on the budget. Entry charges can be varied from day to day to encourage a spread of peak loadings, and are the best means of establishing how interesting and enjoyable a site is. If people are paying to visit the site they will expect value for their money and make known their criticisms. Additional revenue from catering or sales of literature, photos, drawings, guides, souvenirs, etc., can also help to develop the site and benefit its visitors. There may be complaints when entry charges are first introduced; in such cases, it may be advisable to give local people free passes or to allow free entry on one (quiet) day a week, or after a certain hour. The entrance charge could also be voluntary, with an arrangement that those not paying still have to go past the turnstile and staff.

Wherever possible, a single charge should allow access to the whole heritage site, as this produces the most income with least staff cost. If there are different buildings to be entered, a single ticket may be marked at each entry point. If the number of attractions is great, some choices may need to be offered to keep the overall ticket price reasonable, and, in this case, the options available should be clear. Generally, visitor management should take into account physical arrangements and persuasion, with regulations, prohibition signs and policing introduced in a suitable manner.

Visitor management on World Heritage sites involves establishment of a promotion strategy. Attention can be drawn to features that are not likely to be congested, and the preferred times of day to visit the most popular features can be indicated. Advertisements addressing the public, as well as local and international tour operators, can be confined to certain seasons, or to certain, selected categories within the mass media in order to influence the type of people who come. Reduced rates can be offered to *bona fide* groups interested in aspects of cultural heritage, and special privileges provided for genuinely educational parties.

Long queues for admission to facilities are undesirable since they reduce visitor satisfaction and congest the site and parking lots. A maximum capacity for visitors has to be established and not exceeded. In addition, the feeling of overcrowding can be greatly reduced by sensitivity in the use of visitor-management techniques.

10.4.1 Promotion

Since World Heritage sites constitute important economic and cultural assets, it is inevitable that they will be publicized, advertised and promoted by those whose daily duty or interest this is. If the site management does not have the expertise to do this cost-effectively, it should influence the way it is done in order to gain the greatest advantage for the site and the least disadvantage for its conservation.

For promotional purposes, the heritage site is a product in the world marketplace which has to be described correctly, but glowingly, in order to attract visitors, yet with the type and extent of the facilities available made absolutely clear. Journalistic coverage is much better than advertisements, and hence press visitors should be encouraged. They need to be assisted by the provision of correct information, and a press briefing kit should be available to this end.

The design of all promotional material and advertisements must be of a high standard so as to bring credit to the site and its managers. Before any expenditure on promotion is incurred, however, the target audience should be carefully defined and their interests identified.

10.4.2   A code of practice

It is essential to establish a balance between the development of tourism and conservation of World Cultural Heritage and to coordinate efforts for their mutual benefit. The Director General of the National Trust of England, Mr A. Stirling, in his address to the ICOMOS conference in Canterbury, U.K. in 1990, proposed the following Code of Practice for the resources in his care:

> 1. Comprehensive tourist development plans are essential as the pre-condition for developing any tourist potential.
>
> 2. It should be a fundamental principle of any tourist development plan that both conservation, in its widest sense, and tourism benefit from it. This principle should be part of the constitutional purpose of all national tourist agencies, and of local authority tourism and recreation departments.
>
> 3. A significant proportion of revenue earned from tourism should be applied for the benefit of conservation, both nationally and regionally.
>
> 4. The best long-term interests of the people living and working in any host community should be the primary determining factor in selecting options for tourist development.
>
> 5. Educational programmes should assist and invite tourists to respect and understand the local way of life, culture, history and religion. Tourism policy should take these factors into account.
>
> 6. The design of new buildings, sites and transport systems should minimize the potentially harmful visual effects of tourism. Pollution controls should be built into all forms of infrastructure. Where sites of great natural beauty are concerned, the intrusion of man-made structures should be avoided if possible.
>
> 7. Good management should define the level of acceptable tourism development and provide controls to maintain that level.

These principles are equally applicable to World Heritage sites, and valid for consideration in the development of any Management Plan.

REFERENCES

ANON. 1983. *The Secretary of the Interior's Standards for Rehabilitation and Guidelines for Rehabilitating Historic Buildings.* Revised 1983. US Dept. Interior, National Parks Service, Washington D.C. [US Govt Printing Office ref: 1983: 0-416-688]

ASHURST, J. & ASHURST, N. 1988. *Practical Building Conservation.* Vol. 1: Stone Masonry [ISBN 0 291 39745 X]; Vol. 2: Brick Terracotta and Earth [ISBN 0 291 39746 8]; Vol. 3: Mortars, Plasters and Renders [ISBN 0 291 39747 6]; Vol. 4: Metals [ISBN 0 291 39748 4]; Vol. 5: Wood, Glass and Resins, and Technical Bibliography [ISBN 0 291 39776 X]. English Heritage Technical Handbook series. Aldershot, UK: Gower Technical Press.

BECKMANN, POUL. 1995. *Structural Aspects of Building Conservation.* International Series in Structural Engineering. London: McGraw-Hill.

BIANCA, S., DAVID, J-C., QUDSI, A., RIZZARDI, G., BETON, Y., & CHAUFFERT-YVART, B. 1980. *The Conservation of the Old City of Aleppo.* Report prepared by UNESCO for the Government of the Syrian Arab Republic. UNESCO report ref. PP/1979-80/4/7.6/05 FMR/CC/CH/80/139 (Bianca, etc.)

BRANDI, C. 1963. *Teoria del restauro.* Rome: Ediz. Storia e Letteratura.

CERVELLATI, P.L., SCANNAVINI, R., & DE ANGELIS, C. 1977. *La nuova cultura delle città.* Milan: Mondadori.

CESARI, C. 1982. *Considerations on the Problems of Integrated Conservation.* Lecture notes, ICCROM course in Architectural Conservation.

CLEERE, H. (ed.) 1989. *Archaeological Heritage Management in the Modern World.* [One World Archaeology series, vol. 9] London: Unwin Hyman.

————. 1996. Protecting the world's cultural heritage. In: Marks, S. (ed.) *Concerning Buildings. Studies in Honour of Sir Bernard Feilden,* 82-95. London: Butterworths.

COUNCIL OF EUROPE. 1975. "Declaration of Amsterdam." The European Charter of the Architectural Heritage, adopted by the Committee of Ministers of the Council of Europe, 26 September 1975, and solemnly proclaimed at the Congress on the European Architectural Heritage, Amsterdam, The Netherlands, 21-25 October 1975.

FEILDEN, Sir Bernard M. 1982. *Conservation of Historic Buildings.* Technical Studies in the Arts, Archaeology and Architecture series. London: Butterworth Scientific. ISBN 0 408 10782 0

———— 1987. *Between Two Earthquakes: Cultural Property in Seismic Zones.* Los Angeles, CA: The Getty Conservation Institute & ICCROM. ISBN 0 89236 128 X

FIRE PROTECTION ASSOCIATION. No date. *Heritage under fire: A guide to the protection of historic buildings.* Publ. by the Fire Protection Assoc., 140 Aldersgate St., London EC1A 4HX, UK, on behalf of the UK Working Party on Fire Safety in Historic Buildings. ISBN 0 902167 94 4

FITCH, J.M. 1982. *Historic Preservation: Curatorial Management of the Built World.* New York, NY: McGraw-Hill.

HOLLY, M.A. 1984. *Panofsky and the Foundations of Art History.* Ithaca, NY: Cornell Univ. Press.

ICCROM. 1983. [The UNESCO, ICCROM & ICOMOS] *International Meeting of Coordinators of Training in Architectural Conservation/Reunion internationale des coordinateurs pour la formation en conservation architecturale.* Rome, 2-4 December 1982 [In English and French] Rome: ICCROM.

ICCROM-GCI. 1994. *International Directory on Training in Conservation of Cultural Heritage.* Los Angeles: The Getty Conservation Institute & ICCROM.

ICOMOS 1971. The "Venice Charter." [International Charter for the Conservation and Restoration of Monuments and Sites.] Adopted at "The Monument for the Man," the 2nd International Congress of Restoration, Venice, 25-31 May 1964. Padova, Italy: Marsilio Editori on behalf of ICOMOS.

ICOMOS. 1987. *The International Charter for the Conservation of Historic Towns and Urban Areas.* Adopted at "Old Cultures in New Worlds," The [ICOMOS] 8th General Assembly and International Symposium, Washington D.C., 10-15 October 1987. Washington, D.C.: ICOMOS.

JOKILEHTO, J. 1986. A history of architectural conservation: the contribution of English, French, German and Italian thought towards an international approach to the conservation of cultural property. D.Phil. Thesis, Univ. York, UK.

————. 1996. International standards, principles and charters of conservation. In: Marks, S. (ed.) *Concerning Buildings. Studies in Honour of Sir Bernard Feilden*, 55-81. London: Butterworths.

LARSEN, K.E. (ed.) 1995. *Nara Conference on Authenticity in relation to the World Heritage Convention. Nara, Japan, 1-6 November 1994. Proceedings.* UNESCO World Heritage Centre, Angency for Cultural Affairs (Japan), ICCROM and ICOMOS. Trondheim, Norway: Tapir Publishers.

LARSEN, K.E., & MARSTEIN, N. (eds.) 1992. Proc. *International Symposium on Fire Protection of Historic Buildings and Towns*, Risør, Norway, 12-14 September 1990. Publ. by Tapir Forlag, on behalf of Central Office of Historic Monuments and Sites, Norway, and The Norwegian Institute of Technology, in cooperation with the ICOMOS International Wood Committee.

———— 1995. *Conference on authenticity in relation to the World Heritage Convention. Preparatory Workshop, Bergen, Norway, 31 January-2 February 1994. Workshop Proceedings.* Riksantikvaren (Directorate for Cultural Heritage), Norway. Norway: Tapir Forlag.

MARKS, S. (ed.) 1996. *Concerning Buildings. Studies in Honour of Sir Bernard Feilden.* London: Butterworths.

MORA, P., MORA, L., & PHILIPPOT, P. 1977. *La conservation des peintures murales.* Bologna: Editrice Compositori, for ICCROM. Published in 1984 in English as The Conservation of Wall Paintings. London: Butterworths. ISBN 0 408 10812 6

ORGAN, R.M. 1975. The Organisation of an integrated facility for conservation. *Bulletin de l'Institut Royal du Patrimoine Artistique*, **15**: 283-301.

RIEGL, A. 1903. *Der Moderne Denkmalkultus, sein Wesen, seine Entstehung.* Vienna. English translation published in 1982 as Modern cult of monuments: its character and its origin. *Oppositions*, **25**: 20-51.

SEASE, C. 1987. *A Conservation Manual for the Field Archaeologist* Archaeological Research Tools, Vol. 4. Institute of Archaeology, UCLA. ISBN 0 917956 59 1

SIRAVO, F., & PULVER, A. 1986. *Planning Lamu: Conservation of an East African Seaport.* Nairobi: The National Museums of Kenya.

STOVEL, H. 1991. Safeguarding historic urban ensembles in a time of change: A management guide. Draft distributed as a working document for comment at the *International Symposium on World Heritage Towns*, Quebec, Canada, 1991.

UNESCO. 1972. Convention concerning the Protection of the World Cultural and Natural Heritage.

———— 1977 (Revised 1997). Operational Guidelines for the Implementation of the World Heritage Convention.

———— 1985. *Conventions and Recommendations of Unesco concerning the protection of the cultural heritage.* Paris: UNESCO. ISBN: (English) 92 3 102101 X; (French) 92 3 202101 3

UNITED NATIONS. 1987. *Our Common Future.* Oxford: Oxford Univ. Press on behalf of the [UN] World Commission on Environment and Development.

von DROSTE, B., PLACHTER, J. & RÖSSLER, M. (eds.) 1995. *Cultural Landscapes of Universal Value – Components of a Global Strategy.* Germany: Gustav Fischer.

Appendix A
International Charter for the Conservation and Restoration of Monuments and Sites

"The Charter of Venice" (Venice, May 1964)

Imbued with a message from the past, the historic monuments of generations of people remain to the present day as living witnesses of their age-old traditions. People are becoming more and more conscious of the unity of human values and regard ancient monuments as a common heritage. The common responsibility to safeguard them for future generations is recognized. It is our duty to hand them on in the full richness of their authenticity.

It is essential that the principles guiding the preservation and restoration of ancient buildings should be agreed and be laid down on an international basis, with each country being responsible for applying the plan within the framework of its own culture and traditions.

By defining these basic principles for the first time, the Athens Charter of 1931 contributed towards the development of an extensive international movement which has assumed concrete form in national documents, in the work of ICOM and Unesco and in the establishment by the latter of the International Centre for the Study of the Preservation and the Restoration of Cultural Property. Increasing awareness and critical study have been brought to bear on problems which have continually become more complex and varied; now the time has come to examine the Charter afresh in order to make a thorough study of the principles involved and to enlarge its scope in a new document.

Accordingly, the 2nd International Congress of Architects and Technicians of Historic Monuments, which met in Venice from May 25th to 31st 1964, approved the following text:

DEFINITIONS

Article 1. The Concept of an historic monument embraces not only the single architectural work but also the urban or rural setting in which is found the evidence of a particular civilization, a significant development or an historic event. This applies not only to great works of art but also to more modest works of the past which have acquired cultural significance with the passing of time.

Article 2. The conservation and restoration of monuments must have recourse to all the sciences and techniques which can contribute to the study and safeguarding of the architectural heritage.

Article 3. The intention in conserving and restoring monuments is to safeguard them no less as works of art than as historical evidence.

CONSERVATION

Article 4. It is essential to the conservation of monuments that they be maintained on a permanent basis.

Article 5. The conservation of monuments is always facilitated by making use of them for some socially useful purpose. Such use is therefore desirable but it must not change the lay-out or decoration of the building. It is within these limits only that modifications demanded by a change of function should be envisaged and may be permitted.

Article 6. The conservation of a monument implies preserving a setting which is not out of scale. Wherever the traditional setting exists, it must be kept. No new construction, demolition or modification which would alter the relation of mass and colour must be allowed.

Article 7. A monument is inseparable from the history to which it bears witness and from the setting in which it occurs. The moving of all or part of a monument cannot be allowed except where it is justified by national or international interests of paramount importance.

Article 8. Items of sculpture, painting or decoration which form an integral part of a monument may only be removed from it if this is the sole means of ensuring their preservation.

RESTORATION

Article 9. The process of restoration is a highly specialized operation. Its aim is to preserve and reveal the aesthetic and historic value of the monument and is based on respect for original material and authentic documents. It must stop at the point where conjecture begins, and in this case, moreover, any extra work which is indispensable must be distinct from the architectural composition and must bear a contemporary stamp. The restoration in any case must be preceded and followed by an archaeological and historical study of the monument.

Article 10. Where traditional techniques prove inadequate, the consolidation of a monument can be achieved by the use of any modern technique for conservation and construction, the efficacy of which has been shown by scientific data and proved by experience.

Article 11. The valid contributions of all periods to the building of a monument must be respected, since unity of style is not the aim of a restoration. When a building includes the superimposed work of different periods, the revealing of the underlying state can only be justified in exceptional circumstances and when what is removed is of little interest and the material which is brought to light is of great historical, archaeological or aesthetic value, and its state of preservation good enough to justify the action. Evaluation of the importance of the elements involved and the decision as to what may be destroyed cannot rest solely on the individual in charge of the work.

Article 12. Replacements of missing parts must integrate harmoniously with the whole, but at the same time must be distinguishable from the original so that restoration does not falsify the artistic or historic evidence.

Article 13. Additions cannot be allowed except in so far as they do not detract from the interesting parts of the building, its traditional setting, the balance of its composition and its relation with its surroundings.

HISTORIC SITES

Article 14. The sites of monuments must be the object of special care in order to safeguard their integrity and ensure that they are cleared and presented in a seemly manner. The work of conservation and restoration carried out in such places should be inspired by the principles set forth in the foregoing articles.

EXCAVATIONS

Article 15. Excavations should be carried out in accordance with scientific standards and the recommendation defining international principles to be applied in the case of archaeological excavation adopted by UNESCO in 1956.

Ruins must be maintained and measures necessary for the permanent conservation and protection of architectural features and of objects discovered must be taken. Furthermore, every means must be taken to facilitate the understanding of the monument and to reveal it without ever distorting its meaning.

All reconstruction work should however be ruled out *a priori*. Only anastylosis, that is to say, the re-assembling of existing but dismembered parts can be permitted. The material used for integration should always be recognizable and its use should be the least that will ensure the conservation of a monument and the reinstatement of its form.

PUBLICATION

Article 16. In all works of preservation, restoration or excavation, there should always be precise documentation in the form of analytical and critical reports, illustrated with drawings and photographs.

Every stage of the work of clearing, consolidation, rearrangement and integration, as well as technical and formal features identified during the course of the work, should be included. This record should be placed in the archives of a public institution and made available to research workers. It is recommended that the report should be published.

The following persons took part in the work of the Committee for drafting the International Charter for the Conservation and Restoration of Monuments:

Mr Piero GAZZOLA, Chairman	(Italy)
Mr Raymond LEMAIRE, Rapporteur	(Belgium)
Mr José BASSEGODA-NONELL	(Spain)
Mr Luis BENAVENTE	(Portugal)
Mr Djurdje BOSKOVIC	(Yugoslavia)
Mr Hiroshi DAIFUKU	(UNESCO)
Mr P.L. DE VRIEZE	(Netherlands)
Mr Harald LANGBERG	(Denmark)
Mr Mario MATTEUCCI	(Italy)
Mr Jean MERLET	(France)
Mr Carlos FLORES MARINI	(Mexico)
Mr Roberto PANE	(Italy)
Mr S.C.J. PAVEL	(Czechoslovakia)
Mr Paul PHILIPPOT	(ICCROM)
Mr Victor PIMENTEL	(Peru)
Mr Harold J. PLENDERLEITH	(ICCROM)
Mr Deoclecio REDIG DE CAMPOS	(Vatican)
Mr Jean SONNIER	(France)
Mr François SORLIN	(France)
Mr Eustathios STIKAS	(Greece)
Mrs Gertrud TRIPP	(Austria)
Mr Jan ZACHWATOVICZ	(Poland)
Mr Mustafa S. ZBISS	(Tunisia)

Preamble

1. We, the experts assembled in Nara, Japan, wish to acknowledge the generous spirit and intellectual courage of the Japanese authorities in providing a timely forum in which we could challenge conventional thinking in the conservation field, and debate ways and means of broadening our horizons to bring greater respect for cultural and heritage diversity to conservation practice.

2. We also wish to acknowledge the value of the framework for discussion provided by the World Heritage Committee's desire to apply the test of authenticity in ways which accord full respect to the social and cultural values of all societies, in examining the outstanding universal value of cultural properties proposed for the World Heritage List.

3. The Nara Document on Authenticity is conceived in the spirit of the Charter of Venice, 1964, and builds on it and extends it in response to the expanding scope of cultural heritage concerns and interests in our contemporary world.

4. In a world that is increasingly subject to the forces of globalization and homogenization, and in a world where the search for cultural identity is sometimes pursued through aggressive nationalism and the suppression of the cultures of minorities, the essential contribution made by the consideration of authenticity in conservation practice is to clarify and illuminate the collective memory of humanity.

Cultural diversity and heritage diversity

1. The diversity of cultures and heritage in our world is an irreplaceable source of spiritual and intellectual richness for all humankind. The protection and enhancement of cultural and heritage diversity in our world should be actively promoted as an essential aspect of human development.

2. Cultural heritage diversity exists in time and space, and demands respect for other cultures and all aspects of their belief systems. In cases where cultural values appear to be in conflict, respect for cultural diversity demands acknowledgement of the legitimacy of the cultural values of all parties.

3. All cultures and societies are rooted in the particular forms and means of tangibles and intangible expression which constitute their heritage, and these should be respected.

4. It is important to underline a fundamental principle of UNESCO, to the effect that the cultural heritage of each is the cultural heritage of all. Responsibility for cultural heritage and the management of it belongs, in the first place, to the cultural community that has generated it, and subsequently, to that which cares for it. Adherence to the international charters and conventions developed for conservation of cultural heritage obliges consideration of the principles and responsibilities flowing from them. Balancing their own requirements with those of other cultural communities is, for each community, highly desirable, provided achieving this balance does not undermine their fundamental cultural values.

Values and authenticity

1. Conservation of cultural heritage in all its forms and historical periods is rooted in the values attributed to the heritage. Our ability to understand these values depends, in part, on the degree to which information sources about these values may be understood as credible or truthful. Knowledge and understanding of these sources of information, in relation to original and subsequent characteristics of the cultural heritage, and their meaning, is a requisite basis for assessing all aspects of authenticity.

2. Authenticity, considered in this way and affirmed in the Charter of Venice, appears as the essential qualifying factor concerning values. The understanding of authenticity plays a fundamental role in all scientific studies of cultural heritage, in conservation and restoration planning, as well as within the inscription procedures used for the World Heritage Convention and other cultural heritage inventories.

3. All judgements about values attributed to heritage as well as the credibility of related information sources may differ from culture to culture, and even within the same culture. It is thus not possible to base judgements of value and authenticity on fixed criteria. On the contrary, the respect due to all cultures requires that cultural heritage must be considered and judged within the cultural contexts to which it belongs.

4. Therefore, it is of the highest importance and urgency that, within each culture, recognition be accorded to the specific nature of its heritage values and the credibility and truthfulness of related information sources.

5. Depending on the nature of the cultural heritage, its cultural context, and its evolution through time, authenticity judgements may be linked to the worth of a great variety of sources of information. Aspects of these sources may include form and design, materials and substance, use and function, traditions and techniques, location and setting, and spirit and feeling, and other internal and external factors. The use of these sources permits elaboration of the specific artistic, historic, social and scientific dimensions of the cultural heritage being examined.

Definitions

Conservation: all operations designed to understand a property, know its history and meaning, ensure its material safeguard and, if required, its restoration and enhancement.

Information sources: all monumental, written, oral and figurative sources which make it possible to know the nature, specificities, meaning and history of a property.

N.B.: This text was adopted at the close of the Nara Conference with some subsequent editing to harmonize the English and French editions, published in: Larsen, K.E. (ed.). *Nara Conference on Authenticity, Conference de Nara sur l'Authenticité, Japan / Japon 1994, Proceedings / Compte-rendu*, UNESCO, ICCROM, ICOMOS, Agency for Cultural Affairs, Japan, 1995: xxi-xxv.

Conventions and Recommendations of UNESCO
concerning the protection of the cultural heritage

A. Conventions

- Convention for the Protection of Cultural Property in the Event of Armed Conflict (the 'Hague Convention'), with Regulations for the Execution of the Convention, as well as the Protocol to the Convention and the Conference Resolutions,
  14 May 1954

- Convention on the Means of Prohibiting and Preventing the Illicit Import, Export and Transfer of Ownership of Cultural Property,
  14 November 1970

- Convention concerning the Protection of the World Cultural and Natural Heritage,
  16 November 1972

B. Recommendations

- Recommendation on International Principles Applicable to Archaeological Excavations,
  5 December 1956

- Recommendation concerning the most Effective Means of Rendering Museums Accessible to Everyone,
  14 December 1960

- Recommendation concerning the Safeguarding of the Beauty and Character of Landscapes and Sites,
  11 December 1962

- Recommendation on the Means of Prohibiting and Preventing the Illicit Export, Import and Transfer of Ownership of Cultural Property,
  19 November 1964

- Recommendation concerning the Preservation of Cultural Property Endangered by Public or Private Works,
  19 November 1968

- Recommendation concerning the Protection, at National Level, of the Cultural and Natural Heritage,
  16 November 1972

- Recommendation concerning the International Exchange of
  Cultural Property,
  26 November 1976
- Recommendation concerning the Safeguarding and Contemporary
  Role of Historic Areas,
  26 November 1976
- Recommendation for the Protection of Movable Cultural Property,
  28 November 1978
- Recommendation for the Safeguarding and Preservation of Moving Images,
  27 October 1980

Appendix D
World Cultural Heritage Sites

As of December 1997, 552 properties in 111 countries had been included in the World Heritage List. The 418 cultural sites (c) and 20 mixed cultural and natural sites (m) are given below. The first dates given are those of the original inclusion; subsequent dates refer to extensions or other modifications of the site boundaries. Sites in italics are on the List of World Heritage in Danger.

ALBANIA

Butrinti, 1992, c

ALGERIA

Al Qal'a of Beni Hammad, 1980, c
Tassili n'Ajjer, 1982, m
M'Zab Valley, 1982, c
Djémila, 1982, c
Tipasa, 1982, c
Timgad, 1982, c
Kasbah of Algiers, 1992, c

ARGENTINA and BRAZIL

Jesuit Missions of the Guaranis: San Ignacio Mini, Santa Ana, Nuestra Señora de Loreto and Santa Maria Mayor (Argentina); Ruins of Sao Miguel das Missoes (Brazil); 1983-1984, c

ARMENIA

The Monastery of Haghpat, 1996, c

AUSTRALIA

Kakadu National Park, 1981, 1987, 1992, m
Willandra Lakes Region, 1981, m
Tasmanian Wilderness, 1982, m
Uluru-Kata Tjuta National Park, 1994, m

AUSTRIA

The Historic Centre of the City of Salzburg, 1996, c
The Palace and Gardens of Schönbrun, 1996, c
Hallstatt-Dachstein Salzkammergut Cultural Landscape, 1997, c

BANGLADESH

The Historic Mosque City of Bagerhat, 1985, c
Ruins of the Buddhist Vihara at Paharpur, 1985, c

BENIN

Royal Palaces of Abomey, 1985, c

BOLIVIA

City of Potosi, 1987, c
Jesuit Missions of the Chiquitos, 1990, c
Historic City of Sucre, 1991, c

BRAZIL

Historic Town of Ouro Preto, 1980, c
Historic Centre of the Town of Olinda, 1982, c
Historic Centre of Salvador de Bahia, 1985, c
Sanctuary of Bom Jesus do Congonhas, 1985, c
Brasilia, 1987, c
Serra da Capivara National Park, 1991, c
Historic Centre of Sao Luis, 1997, c

BULGARIA

Boyana Church, 1979, c
Madara Rider, 1979, c
Rock-hewn Churches of Ivanovo, 1979, c
Thracian Tomb of Kazanlak, 1979, c
Ancient City of Nessebar, 1983, c
Rila Monastery, 1983, c
Thracian Tomb of Sveshtari, 1985, c

CAMBODIA

Angkor, 1992, c

CANADA

L'Anse aux Meadows National Historic Park, 1978, c
Anthony Island, 1981, c
Head-Smashed-In Buffalo Jump, 1981, c
Quebec (Historic Area), 1985, c
Lunenburg Old Town, 1995, c

CHILE

Rapa Nui National Park, 1995, c

CHINA

The Great Wall, 1987, c
Mount Taishan, 1987, m
Imperial Palace of the Ming and Qing Dynasties, 1987, c
Mogao Caves, 1987, c
The Mausoleum of the First Qin Emperor, 1987, c
Peking Man Site at Zhoukoudian, 1987, c
Mount Huangshan, 1990, m
The Mountain Resort and its Outlying Temples, Chengde, 1994, c
The Temple and Cemetery of Confucius, and the Kong Family Mansion in Qufu, 1994, c
The ancient building complex in the Wudang Mountains, 1994, c
The Potala Palace, Lhasa, 1994, c
Lushan National Park, 1996, c
Mt. Emei and Leshan Giant Buddha, 1996, m
The Old Town of Lijiang, 1997, c
The Ancient City of Ping Yao, 1997, c
The Classical Gardens of Suzhou, 1997, c

COLOMBIA

Port, Fortresses and Group of Monuments, Carthagena, 1984, c
Historic Centre of Santa Cruz de Mompox, 1995, c
National Archaeological Park of Tierradentro, 1995, c
San Agustin Archaeological Park, 1995, c

CROATIA

Old City of Dubrovnik, 1979/1994, c
Historical Complex of Split with the Palace of Diocletian, 1979, c
The Episcopal Complex of the Euphrasian Basilica in the Historic Centre of Porec, 1997, c
The Historic City of Trogir, 1997, c

CUBA

Old Havana and its Fortifications, 1982, c
Trinidad and the Valley de los Ingenios, 1988, c
San Pedro de la Roca Castle, Santiago de Cuba, 1997, c

CYPRUS

Paphos, 1980, c
Painted Churches in the Troodos Region, 1985, c

CZECH REPUBLIC

Historic Centre of Prague, 1992, c
Historic Centre of Cesky Krumlov, 1992, c
Historic Centre of Telc, 1992, c

Pilgrimage Church of St. John of Nepomuk at Zelena Hora, 1994, c
Kutna Hora – the Historical Town Centre with the Church of Saint Barbara and the Cathedral of our Lady at Sedlec, 1995, c
The Lednice-Valtice Cultural Landscape, 1996, c

DENMARK

Jelling Mounds, Runic Stones and Church, 1994, c
Roskilde Cathedral, 1995, c

DOMINICAN REPUBLIC

Colonial City of Santo Domingo, 1990, c

ECUADOR

Old City of Quito, 1978, c

EGYPT

Ancient Thebes with its Necropolis, 1979, c
Islamic Cairo, 1979, c
Memphis and its Necropolis - the Pyramid Fields from Giza to Dahshur, 1979, c
Nubian Monuments from Abu Simbel to Philae, 1979, c
Abu Mena, 1979, c

EL SALVADOR

Joya de Ceren Archaeological Site, 1993, c

ESTONIA

The Historic Centre (Old Town) of Tallinn, 1997, c

ETHIOPIA

Rock-hewn Churches of Lalibela, 1978, c
Fasil Ghebbi, Gondar Region, 1979, c
Aksum 1980, c
Lower Valley of the Awash, 1980, c
Lower Valley of the Omo, 1980, c
Tiya, 1980, c

FINLAND

Old Rauma, 1991, c
Fortress of Suomenlinna, 1991, c
Petäjävesi Old Church, 1994, c
Verla Groundwood and Board Mill, 1996, c

FORMER YUGOSLAV REPUBLIC OF MACEDONIA

Ohrid Region, including its cultural and historical aspects and its natural environment, 1980, m

FRANCE

Mont-Saint-Michel and its Bay, 1979, c

Chartres Cathedral, 1979, c
Palace and Park of Versailles, 1979, c
Vézelay, Church and Hill, 1979, c
Decorated Grottoes of the Vézère Valley, 1979, c
Palace and Park of Fontainebleau, 1981, c
Château and Estate of Chambord, 1981, c
Amiens Cathedral, 1981, c
The Roman Theatre, its Surroundings and the
    Triumphal Arch of Orange, 1981, c
Roman and Romanesque Monuments of Arles,
    1981, c
Cistercian Abbey of Fontenay, 1981, c
Royal Saltworks of Arc-et-Senans, 1982, c
Place Stanislas, Place de la Carrière and Place
    d'Alliance in Nancy, 1983, c
Church of Saint-Savin sur Gartempe, 1983, c
Pont du Gard (Roman aqueduct), 1985, c
Strasbourg - Grande Ile, 1988, c
Paris, Banks of the Seine, 1991, c
Cathedral of Notre-Dame, former Abbey of
    Saint-Remi and Tau Palace, of Reims, 1991, c
Bourges Cathedral, 1992, c
Historic Centre of Avignon, 1995, c
Le Canal du Midi, 1996, c
The Historic Fortified City of Carcassonne,
    1997, c

FRANCE/SPAIN

Pyrenees - Mount Perdu, 1997, m

GEORGIA

The City-Museum Reserve of Mtskheta, 1994, c
Bagrati Cathedral and Gelati Monastery, 1994, c
Upper Svaneti, 1996, c

GERMANY

Aachen Cathedral, 1978, c
Speyer Cathedral, 1981, c
Würzburg Residence with the Court Gardens and
    Residence Square, 1981, c
Pilgrimage Church of Wies, 1983, c
The Castles of Augustusburg and Falkenlust at
    Brühl, 1984, c
St. Mary's Cathedral and St. Michael's Church
    at Hildesheim, 1985, c
Roman Monuments, Cathedral and
    Liebfrauen-Church in Trier, 1986, c
Hanseatic City of Lübeck, 1987, c
Palaces and Parks of Potsdam and Berlin, 1990, c
Abbey and Altenmünster of Lorsch, 1991, c
Mines of Rammelsberg and the Historic Town of
    Goslar, 1992, c
Town of Bamberg, 1993, c
Maulbronn Monastery Complex, 1993, c

The Collegiate Church, Castle, and old Town of
    Quedlinburg, 1994, c
Völklingen Ironworks, 1994, c
Cologne Cathedral, 1996, c
The Bauhaus and its sites in Weimar and Dessau,
    1996, c
The Luther Memorials in Eisleben and
    Wittenberg, 1996, c

GHANA

Forts and Castles, Volta, Greater Accra, Central
    and Western Regions, 1979, c
Ashante Traditional Buildings, 1980, c

GREECE

Temple of Apollo Epicurius at Bassae, 1986, c
Archaeological Site of Delphi, 1987, c
The Acropolis, Athens, 1987, c
Mount Athos, 1988, m
Meteora, 1988, m
Paleochristian and Byzantine Monuments
    of Thessalonika, 1988, c
Archaeological Site of Epidaurus, 1988, c
Mediaeval City of Rhodes, 1988, c
Archaeological Site of Olympia, 1989, c
Mystras, 1989, c
Delos, 1990, c
Monasteries of Daphni, Hossios Luckas, and
    Nea Moni of Chios, 1990, c
Pythagoreion and Heraion of Samos, 1992, c
The Archaeological Site of Vergina, 1996, c

GUATEMALA

Antigua Guatemala, 1979, c
Tikal National Park, 1979, m
Archaeological Park and Ruins of Quirigua,
    1981, c

HAITI

Citadel, Sans Souci Palace, and Ramiers National
    Historic Park, 1982, c

HOLY SEE

Vatican City, 1984, c

HONDURAS

Maya Site of Copan, 1980, c

HUNGARY

Budapest, the Banks of the Danube with the
    district of Buda Castle, 1987, c
Hollókö, 1987, c
The Millenary Benedictine Abbey of
    Pannonhalma and its Natural Environment,
    1996, c

INDIA

Ajanta Caves, 1983, c
Ellora Caves, 1983, c
Agra Fort, 1983, c
Taj Mahal, 1983, c
The Sun Temple, Konarak, 1984, c
Group of Monuments at Mahabalipuram, 1984, c
Churches and Convents of Goa, 1986, c
Group of Monuments at Khajuraho, 1986, c
Group of Monuments at Hampi, 1986, c
Fatehpur Sikri, 1986, c
Group of Monuments at Pattadakal, 1987, c
Elephanta Caves, 1987, c
Brihadisvara Temple, Thanjavur, 1987, c
Buddhist Monuments at Sanchi, 1989, c
Humayun's Tomb, Delhi, 1993, c
Qutb Minar and its monuments, Delhi, 1993, c

INDONESIA

Borodubur Temple compound, 1991, c
Prambanan Temple compound, 1991, c
Sangiran Early Man Site, 1996, c

IRAN

Persepolis, 1979, c
Tchogha Zanbil Ziggurat and complex, 1979, c
Meidan Emam, Esfahan, 1979, c

IRAQ

Hatra, 1985, c

IRELAND

Archaeological ensemble of the Bend of the
    Boyne, 1993, c
Skellig Michael, 1996, c

ITALY

Rock Drawings in Valcamonica, 1979, c
The Church and Dominican Convent of Santa
    Maria delle Grazie with 'The Last Supper' by
    Leonardo da Vinci, 1980, c
Historic Centre of Florence, 1982, c
Venice and its Lagoon, 1987, c
Piazza del Duomo, Pisa, 1987, c
Historic Centre of San Gimignano, 1990, c
I Sassi di Matera, 1993, c
The City Of Vicenza and the Palladian Villas of
    the Veneto, 1994/1996, c
Historic Centre of Siena, 1995, c
Historic Centre of Naples, 1995, c
Crespi d'Adda, 1995, c
Ferrara, City of the Renaissance, 1995, c
Castel del Monte, 1996, c
The *Trulli* of Alberobello, 1996, c

The Early Christian Monuments and Mosaics of
    Ravenna, 1996, c
The Historic Centre of the City of Pienza, 1996, c
The 18th-Century Royal Palace at Caserta with
    the Park, the Aqueduct of Vanvitelli, and the
    San Leucio Complex, 1997, c
The Residences of the Royal House of Savoy,
    1997, c
The Botanical Garden (Orto Botanico), Padua,
    1997, c
The Cathedral, Torre Civica and Piazza Grande,
    Modena, 1997, c
The Archaeological Areas of Pompei, Ercolano,
    and Torre Annunziata, 1997, c
Villa Romana del Casale, 1997, c
Su Nuraxi di Barumini, 1997, c
Portovenere, Cinque Terre, and the Islands
    (Palmaria,Tino and Tinetto, 1997, c
The Costiera Amalfitana, 1997, c
The Archaeological Area of Agrigento, 1997, c

ITALY/HOLY SEE

Historic Centre of Rome, the properties of the
    Holy See in that city enjoying extraterritorial
    rights, and San Paolo Fuori le Mura,
    1980/1990, c

JAPAN

Buddhist Monuments in the Horyu-ji area,
    1993, c
Himeji-jo, 1993, c
Historic Monuments of Ancient Kyoto (Kyoto,
    Uji and Otsu Cities), 1994, c
Historic Villages of Shirakawa-go and
    Gokayama, 1995, c
Hiroshima Peace Memorial (Genbaku Dome),
    1996, c
Itsukushima Shinto Shrine, 1996, c

JERUSALEM

*Old City of Jerusalem and its Walls (site
    proposed by Jordan), 1981, c*

JORDAN

Petra, 1985, c
Quseir Amra, 1985, c

LAO PEOPLE'S DEMOCRATIC REPUBLIC

Town of Luang Prabang, 1995, c

LATVIA

The Historic Centre of Riga, 1997, c

LEBANON

Anjar, 1984, c
Baalbek, 1984, c
Byblos, 1984, c
Tyre, 1984, c

LIBYAN ARAB JAMAHIRIYA

Archaeological Site of Leptis Magna, 1982, c
Archaeological Site of Sabratha, 1982, c
Archaeological Site of Cyrene, 1982, c
Rock-art Sites of Tadrart Acacus, 1985, c
Old Town of Ghadamès, 1986, c

LITHUANIA

Vilnius Historic Centre, 1994, c

LUXEMBOURG

The City of Luxembourg, its old quarters and
fortifications, 1994, c

MALI

Old Towns of Djenné, 1988, c
Timbuktu, 1988, c
Cliffs of Bandiagara (Land of the Dogons),
1989, m

MALTA

Hal Saflieni Hypogeum, 1980, c
City of Valetta, 1980, c
Megalithic Temples , 1980, 1992, c

MAURITANIA

The Ancient *Ksour* of Ouadane, Chinguetti,
Tichitt and Oualata, 1996, c

MEXICO

Pre-Hispanic City and National Park of Palenque,
1987, c
Historic Centre of Mexico City and Xochimilco,
1987, c
Pre-Hispanic City of Teotihuacan, 1987, c
Historic Centre of Oaxaca and Archaeological
Site of Monte Alban, 1987, c
Historic Centre of Puebla, 1987, c
Historic Town of Guanajuato and Adjacent
Mines, 1988, c
Pre-Hispanic City of Chichén-Itza, 1988, c
Historic Centre of Morelia, 1991, c
El Tajin, Pre-Hispanic City, 1992, c
Historic Centre of Zacatecas, 1993, c
Rock Paintings of the Sierra de San Francisco,
1993, c
The earliest 16th Century Monasteries on the
slopes of Popocatepetl, 1994, c
The Prehispanic Town of Uxmal, 1996, c
The Historic Monuments Zone of Querétaro,
1996, c
Hospicio Cabanas, Guadalajara, 1997, c

MOROCCO

Medina of Fez, 1981, c
Medina of Marrakesh, 1985, c
Ksar of Aït-Ben-Haddou, 1987, c
The Historic City of Meknes, 1996, c
Medina of Tetouan (formerly known as Titawin),
1997, c
The Archaeological Site of Volubilis, 1997, c

MOZAMBIQUE

Island of Mozambique, 1991, c

NEPAL

Kathmandu Valley, 1979, c
Lumbini, the Birthplace of the Lord Buddha,
1997, c

NETHERLANDS

Schokland and its surroundings, 1995, c
The Defense Line of Amsterdam, 1996, c
The Mill Network at Kinderdijk-Elshout, 1997, c
The Historic Area of Willemstad, Inner City, and
Harbour, Curaçao, 1997, c

NEW ZEALAND

Tongariro National Park, 1990/1993, m

NORWAY

Urnes Stave Church, 1979, c
Bryggen, 1979, c
Røros Mining Town, 1980, c
Rock Drawings of Alta, 1985, c

OMAN

Bahla Fort, 1987, c
Archaeological Sites of Bat, Al-Khutm, and
Al-Ayn, 1988, c

PAKISTAN

Archaeological Ruins at Moenjodaro, 1980, c
Taxila, 1980, c
Buddhist Ruins of Takht-i-Bahi and
Neighbouring City Remains at Sahr-i-Bahlol,
1980, c
Historic Monuments of Thatta, 1981, c
Fort and Shalamar Gardens in Lahore, 1981, c
Rohtas Fort, 1997, c

PANAMA

Fortifications of Portobelo and San Lorenzo,
    1980, c
The Historic District of Panamá, with the Salón
    Bolivar, 1997, c

PARAGUAY

Jesuit Missions of la Santisima Trinidad de
    Parana and Jesus de Tavarangue, 1993, c

PERU

City of Cuzco, 1983, c
Historic Sanctuary of Machu Picchu, 1983, m
Chavin (Archaeological Site), 1985, c
Chan Chan Archaeological Zone, 1986, c
Historic Centre of Lima, 1991, c
Rio Abiseo National Park, 1990/1992, m
The Lines and Geoglyphs of Nasca and Pampas
    de Juma, 1994, c

PHILIPPINES

Baroque Churches of the Philippines, 1993, c
Rice Terraces of the Philippines Cordilleras,
    1995, c

POLAND

Historic Centre of Cracow, 1978, c
Wieliczka Salt Mine, 1978, c
Auschwitz Concentration Camp, 1979, c
Historic Centre of Warsaw, 1980, c
Old City of Zamosc, 1992, c
The Medieval Town of Torun, 1997, c
The Castle of the Teutonic Order in Malbork,
    1997, c

PORTUGAL

Central Zone of the Town of Angra do Heroismo
    in the Azores, 1983, c
Monastery of the Hieronymites and Tower
    of Belem in Lisbon, 1983, c
Monastery of Batalha, 1983, c
Convent of Christ in Tomar, 1983, c
Historic Centre of Evora, 1986, c
Monastery of Alcobaça, 1989, c
Cultural Landscape of Sintra, 1995, c
The Historic Centre of Oporto, 1996, c

REPUBLIC OF KOREA

Sokkuram Grotto and Pulguksa Temple, 1995, c

Haiensa Temple Changgyong P'ango, the
    Depositories for the Tripitaka Koreana
    Woodblocks, 1995, c
The Chongmyo Shrine, 1995, c
The Ch'angdokkung Palace Complex, 1997, c
Hwasong Fortress, 1997, c

ROMANIA

Biertan and its fortified Church, 1993, c
Monastery of Horezu, 1993, c
Churches of Moldavia, 1993, c

RUSSIAN FEDERATION

Historic Centre of Saint Petersburg and related
    groups of monuments*[1], 1990, c
Khizi Pogost*, 1990, c
Kremlin and Red Square in Moscow*, 1990, c
Historic Monuments of Novgorod and
    surroundings, 1992, c
Cultural and Historic Ensemble of the Solovetsky
    Islands, 1992, c
The White Monuments of Vladimir and Suzdal,
    1992, c
Architectural ensemble of the Trinity Sergius
    Lavra in Sergiev Posad, 1993, c
The Church of the Ascension, Kolomenskoye,
    1994, c

SENEGAL

Island of Gorée, 1978, c

SLOVAKIA

Vlkolinec, 1993, c
Banska Stiavnica, 1993, c
Spissky Hrad and its associated cultural
    monuments, 1993, c

SPAIN

The Historic Centre of Córdoba, 1984/1994, c
The Alhambra, Generalife and Albayzin,
    Granada, 1984, c
Burgos Cathedral, 1984, c
Monastery and Site of the Escurial, Madrid,
    1984, c
Parque Güell, Palacio Güell and Casa Mila, in
    Barcelona, 1984, c
Altamira Cave, 1985, c
Old Town of Segovia and its Aqueduct, 1985, c
Churches of the Kingdom of the Asturias, 1985, c
Santiago de Compostela (Old Town), 1985, c
Old Town of Avila with its Extra Muros
    Churches, 1985, c

---

1   The nominations related to the cultural sites marked * were submitted in 1989 by the Union of Soviet
    Socialist Republics.

Mudejar Architecture of Teruel, 1986, c
Historic City of Toledo, 1986, c
Old Town of Caceres, 1986, c
The Cathedral, the Alcazar and the Archivo de
    Indias, Seville, 1987, c
Old City of Salamanca, 1988, c
Poblet Monastery, 1992, c
Archaeological ensemble of Mérida, 1993, c
Royal Monastery of Santa Maria de Guadalupe,
    1993, c
The Route of Santiago de Compostela, 1993, c
The Historic Walled Town of Cuenca, 1996, c
"La Lonja de la Seda" of Valencia, 1996, c
Las Médulas, 1997, c
The Palau de la Musica Catalana and the Hospital
    de Sant Pau, Barcelona, 1997, c
San Millan Yuso and Suso Monasteries, 1997, c

SRI LANKA

Sacred City of Anuradhapura, 1982, c
Ancient City of Polonnaruva, 1982, c
Ancient City of Sigiriya, 1982, c
Sacred City of Kandy, 1988, c
Old Town of Galle and its Fortifications, 1988, c
Golden Temple of Dambulla, 1991, c

SWEDEN

Royal Domain of Drottningholm, 1991, c
Birka and Hovgården, 1993, c
Engelsberg Ironworks, 1993, c
Rock Carvings of Tanum, 1994, c
Skogskyrkogården, 1994, c
Hanseatic Town of Visby, 1995, c
The Church Village of Gammelstad, Luleå,
    1996, c
The Laponian Area, 1996, m

SWITZERLAND

Convent of Saint Gall, 1983, c
Benedictine Convent of Saint John at
    Müstair, 1983, c
Old City of Berne, 1983, c

SYRIAN ARAB REPUBLIC

Ancient City of Damascus, 1979, c
Ancient City of Bosra, 1980, c
Site of Palmyra, 1980, c
Ancient City of Aleppo, 1986, c

THAILAND

Historic Town of Sukhothai and Associated
    Historic Towns, 1991, c
Historic City of Ayutthaya and Associated
    Historic Towns, 1991, c

Ban Chiang Archaeological Site, 1992, c

TUNISIA

Medina of Tunis, 1979, c
Site of Carthage, 1979, c
Amphitheatre of El Djem, 1979, c
Punic Town of Kerkuane and its Necropolis,
    1985, 1986, c
Medina of Sousse, 1988, c
Kairouan, 1988, c
Dougga/Thugga, 1997, c

TURKEY

Historic Areas of Istanbul, 1985, c
Göreme National Park and the Rock Sites
    of Cappadocia, 1985, m
Great Mosque and Hospital of Divrigi, 1985, c
Hattusha, 1986, c
Nemrut Dag, 1987, c
Xanthos-Letoon, 1988, c
Hierapolis-Pamukkale, 1988, m
City of Safranbolu, 1994, c

UKRAINE

Kiev: Saint Sophia Cathedral and related
    monastic buildings, and Lavra of
    Kiev-Pechersk, 1990, c

UNITED KINGDOM

Durham Castle and Cathedral, 1986, c
Ironbridge Gorge, 1986, c
Studley Royal Park including the Ruins of
    Fountains Abbey, 1986, c
Stonehenge, Avebury and Associated Sites,
    1986, c
The Castles and Town Walls of King Edward
    in Gwynedd, 1986, c
Blenheim Palace, 1987, c
City of Bath, 1987, c
Hadrian's Wall, 1987, c
Westminster Palace, Westminster Abbey
    and Saint Margaret's Church, 1987, c
The Tower of London, 1988, c
Canterbury Cathedral, Saint Augustine's Abbey
    and Saint Martin's Church, 1988, c
Old and New Towns of Edinburgh, 1995, c
Maritime Greenwich, 1997, c

UNITED REPUBLIC OF TANZANIA

Ruins of Kilwa Kisiwani and Ruins of Songo
    Mnara, 1981, c

UNITED STATES OF AMERICA

Mesa Verde Naitonal Park, 1978, c
Independence Hall, 1979, c

Cahokia Mounds State Historic Site, 1982, c
La Fortaleza and San Juan Historic Site in
    Puerto Rico, 1983, c
The Statue of Liberty, 1984, c
Chaco Culture National Historic Park, 1987, c
Monticello and University of Virginia in
    Charlottesville, 1987, c
Pueblo de Taos, 1992, c

URUGUAY

Historic Quarter of the City of Colonia del
    Sacramento, 1995, c

UZBEKISTAN

Itchan Kala, 1990, c
Historic Centre of Bukhara, 1993, c

VENEZUELA

Coro and its Port, 1993, c

VIET NAM

Hué (Complex of Monuments), 1993, c

YEMEN

Old Walled City of Shibam, 1982, c
Old City of Sana'a, 1986, c
Historic Town of Zabid, 1993, c

YUGOSLAVIA

Stari Ras and Sopocani, 1979, c
Natural and Culturo-Historical Region of Kotor,
    1979, c
Studenica Monastery, 1986, c

ZIMBABWE

Great Zimbabwe National Monument, 1986, c
Khami Ruins National Monument, 1986, c

Guidelines on Education and Training in the Conservation of Monuments, Ensembles and Sites

The General Assembly of the International Council on Monuments and Sites, ICOMOS, meeting in Colombo, Sri Lanka, at its tenth session from July 30 to August 7, 1993;

Considering the breadth of the heritage encompassed within the concept of *monuments, ensembles and sites*;

Considering the great variety of actions and treatments required for the conservation of these heritage resources, and the necessity of a common discipline for their guidance;

Recognizing that many different professions need to collaborate within the common discipline of conservation in the process and require proper education and training in order to guarantee good communication and coordinated action in conservation;

Noting the Venice Charter and related ICOMOS doctrine, and the need to provide a reference for the institutions and bodies involved in developing training programmes, and to assist in defining and building up appropriate standards and criteria suitable to meet the specific cultural and technical requirements in each community or region;

Adopts the following guidelines, and *Recommends* that they be diffused for the information of appropriate institutions, organizations and authorities.

Aim of the Guidelines

1. The aim of this document is to promote the establishment of standards and guidelines for education and training in the conservation of monuments, groups of buildings (*"ensembles"*) and sites defined as cultural heritage by the World Heritage Convention of 1972. They include historic buildings, historic areas and towns, archaeological sites, and the contents therein, as well as historic and cultural landscapes. Their conservation is now, and will continue to be a matter of urgency.

Conservation

2. Conservation of cultural heritage is now recognized as resting within the general field of environmental and cultural development. Sustainable management strategies for change which respect cultural heritage require the integration of conservation attitudes with contemporary economic and social goals including tourism.

3. The object of conservation is to prolong the life of cultural heritage and, if possible, to clarify the artistic and historical messages therein without the loss of authenticity and meaning. Conservation is a cultural, artistic, technical and craft activity based on humanistic and scientific studies and systematic research. Conservation must respect the cultural context.

Educational and Training Programmes and Courses

4. There is a need to develop a holistic approach to our heritage on the basis of cultural pluralism and diversity, respected by professionals, craftspersons and administrators. Conservation requires the ability to observe, analyze and synthesize. The conservationist should have a flexible yet pragmatic approach based on cultural consciousness which should penetrate all practical work, proper education and training, sound judgement and a sense of proportion with an understanding of the community's needs. Many professional and craft skills are involved in this interdisciplinary activity.

5. Conservation works should only be entrusted to persons competent in these specialist activities. Education and training for conservation should produce from a range of professionals, conservationists who are able to:

   a) read a monument, ensemble or site and identify its emotional, cultural and use significance;

   b) understand the history and technology of monuments, ensembles or sites in order to define their identity, plan for their conservation, and interpret the results of this research;

   c) understand the setting of a monument, ensemble or site, their contents and surroundings, in relation to other buildings, gardens or landscapes;

   d) find and absorb all available sources of information relevant to the monument, ensemble or site being studied;

   e) understand and analyze the behaviour of monuments, ensembles and sites as complex systems;

   f) diagnose intrinsic and extrinsic causes of decay as a basis for appropriate action;

   g) inspect and make reports intelligible to non-specialist readers of monuments, ensembles or sites, illustrated by graphic means such as sketches and photographs;

   h) know, understand and apply Unesco conventions and recommendations, and ICOMOS and other recognized Charters, regulations and guidelines;

   i) make balanced judgements based on shared ethical principles, and accept responsibility for the long-term welfare of cultural heritage;

j) recognize when advice must be sought and define the areas of need of study by different specialists, e.g. wall paintings, sculpture and objects of artistic and historical value, and/or studies of materials and systems;

k) give expert advice on maintenance strategies, management policies and the policy framework for environmental protection and preservation of monuments and their contents, and sites;

l) document works executed and make same accessible.

m) work in multi-disciplinary groups using sound methods;

n) be able to work with inhabitants, administrators and planners to resolve conflicts and to develop conservation strategies appropriate to local needs, abilities and resources;

Aims of Courses

6. There is a need to impart knowledge of conservation attitudes and approaches to all those who may have a direct or indirect impact on cultural property.

7. The practice of conservation is interdisciplinary; it therefore follows that courses should also be multidisciplinary. Professionals, including academics and specialized craftspersons, who have already received their normal qualification will need further training in order to become *conservationists*; equally those who seek to act competently in historic environment.

8. Conservationists should ensure that all artisans and staff working on a monument, ensemble or site respect its significance.

9. Training in disaster preparedness and in methods of mitigating damage to cultural property, by strengthening and improving fire prevention and other security measures, should be included in courses.

10. Traditional crafts are a valuable cultural resource. Craftspersons, already with high level manual skills, should be further trained for conservation work with instruction in the history of their craft, historic details and practices, and the theory of conservation with the need for documentation. Many historic skills will have to be recorded and revived.

Organization of Education and Training

11. Many satisfactory methods of achieving the required education and training are possible. Variations will depend on traditions and legislation, as well as on administrative and economic context of each cultural region. The active exchange of ideas and opinions on new approaches to education and training between national institutes and at international levels should be encouraged. Collaborative network of individuals and institutions is essential to the success of this exchange.

12. Education and sensitization for conservation should begin in schools and continue in universities and beyond. These institutions have an important role in raising

visual and cultural awareness – improving ability to read and understand the elements of our cultural heritage – and giving the cultural preparation needed by candidates for specialist education and training. Practical hands-on training in craft work should be encouraged.

13. Courses for continuing professional development can enlarge on the initial education and training of professionals. Long-term, part-time courses are a valuable method for advanced teaching, and useful in major population centres. Short courses can enlarge attitudes, but cannot teach skills or impart profound understanding of conservation. They can help introduce concepts and techniques of conservation in the management of the built and natural environment and the objects within it.

14. Participants in specialist courses should be of a high calibre normally having had appropriate education and training and practical working experience. Specialist courses should be multi-disciplinary with core subjects for all participants, and optional subjects to extend capacities and/or to fill the gaps in previous education and training. To complete the education and training of a conservationist an internship is recommended to give practical experience.

15. Every country or regional group should be encouraged to develop at least one comprehensively organized institute giving education and training and specialist courses. It may take decades to establish a fully competent conservation service. Special short-term measures may therefore be required, including the grafting of new initiatives onto existing programmes in order to lead to fully developed new programmes. National, regional and international exchange of teachers, experts and students should be encouraged. Regular evaluation of conservation training programmes by peers is a necessity.

Resources

16. Resources needed for specialist courses may include e.g.:

   a) an adequate number of participants of required level ideally in the range of 15 to 25;

   b) a full-time co-ordinator with sufficient administrative support;

   c) instructors with sound theoretical knowledge and practical experience in conservation and teaching ability;

   d) fully equipped facilities including lecture space with audio-visual equipment, video, etc., studios, laboratories, workshops, seminar rooms, and staff offices;

   e) library and documentation centre providing reference collections, facilities for coordinated research, and access to computerized information networks;

   f) a range of monuments, ensembles and sites within a reasonable radius.

17. Conservation depends upon documentation adequate for understanding of monuments, ensembles or sites and their respective settings. Each country should have an institute for research and archive for recording its cultural heritage and all conservation works related thereto. The course should work within the archive responsibilities identified at the national level.

18. Funding for teaching fees and subsistence may need special arrangements for mid-career participants as they may already have personal responsibilities.

(August 1993)

Principles for the Recording of Monuments, Groups of Buildings and Sites

(Text ratified by the 11th ICOMOS General Assembly,
held in Sofia, Bulgaria, from 5 to 9 October 1996)

As the cultural heritage is a unique expression of human achievement; and

as this cultural heritage is continuously at risk; and

as recording is one of the principal ways available to give meaning, understanding, definition and recognition of the values of the cultural heritage; and

as the responsibility for conserving and maintaining the cultural heritage rests not only with the owners but also with conservation specialists and the professionals, managers, politicians and administrators working at all levels of government, and with the public; and

as article 16 of the Charter of Venice requires, it is essential that responsible organisations and individuals record the nature of the cultural heritage.

The purpose of this document is therefore to set out the principal reasons, responsibilities, planning measures, contents, management and sharing considerations for the recording of the cultural heritage.

Definitions of words used in this document:

Cultural Heritage refers to monuments, groups of buildings and sites of heritage value, constituting the historic or built environment.

Recording is the capture of information which describes the physical configuration, condition and use of monuments, groups of buildings and sites, at points in time, and it is an essential part of the conservation process.

Records of monuments, groups of buildings and sites may include tangible as well as intangible evidence, and constitute a part of the documentation that can contribute to an understanding of the heritage and its related values.

The reasons for recording

1. The recording of the cultural heritage is essential:

   a) to acquire knowledge in order to advance the understanding of cultural heritage, its values and its evolution;

b) to promote the interest and involvement of the people in the preservation of the heritage through the dissemination of recorded information;

c) to permit informed management and control of construction works and of all change to the cultural heritage;

d) to ensure that the maintenance and conservation of the heritage is sensitive to its physical form, its materials, construction, and its historical and cultural significance.

2. Recording should be undertaken to an appropriate level of detail in order to:

a) provide information for the process of identification, understanding, interpretation and presentation of the heritage, and to promote the involvement of the public;

b) provide a permanent record of all monuments, groups of buildings and sites that are to be destroyed or altered in any way, or where at risk from natural events or human activities;

c) provide information for administrators and planners at national, regional or local levels to make sensitive planning and development control policies and decisions;

d) provide information upon which appropriate and sustainable use may be identified, and the effective research, management, maintenance programmes and construction works may be planned.

3. Recording of the cultural heritage should be seen as a priority, and should be undertaken especially:

a) when compiling a national, regional, or local inventory;

b) as a fully integrated part of research and conservation activity;

c) before, during and after any works of wrepair, alteration, or other intervention, and when evidence of its history is revealed during such works;

d) when total or partial demolition, destruction, abandonment or relocation is contemplated, or where the heritage is at risk of damage from human or natural external forces;

e) during or following accidental or unforeseen disturbance which damages the cultural heritage;

f) when change of use or responsibility for management or control occurs.

Responsibility for Recording

1. The commitment at the national level to conserve the heritage requires an equal commitment towards the recording process.

2. The complexity of the recording and interpretation processes requires the deployment of individuals with adequate skill, knowledge and awareness for the associated tasks. It may be necessary to initiate training programmes to achieve this.

3. Typically the recording process may involve skilled individuals working in collaboration, such as specialist heritage recorders, surveyors, conservators, architects, engineers, researchers, architectural historians, archaeologists above and below ground, and other specialist advisors.

4. All managers of cultural heritage are responsible for ensuring the adequate recording, quality and updating of the records.

Planning for Recording

1. Before new records are prepared, existing sources of information should be found and examined for their adequacy.

   a) The type of records containing such information should be searched for in surveys, drawings, photographs, published and unpublished accounts and descriptions, and related documents pertaining to the origins and history of the building, group of buildings or site. It is important to search out recent as well as old records;

   b) Existing records should be searched for in locations such as national and local public archives, in professional, institutional or private archives, inventories and collections, in libraries or museums;

   c) Records should be searched for through consultation with individuals and organisations who have owned, occupied, recorded, constructed, conserved, or carried out research into or who have knowledge of the building, group of buildings or site.

2. Arising out of the analysis above, selection of the appropriate scope, level and methods of recording requires that:

   a) The methods of recording and type of documentation produced should be appropriate to the nature of the heritage, the purposes of the record, the cultural context, and the funding or other resources available. Limitations of such resources may require a phased approach to recording. Such methods might include written descriptions and analyses, photographs (aerial or terrestrial), rectified photography, photogrammetry, geophysical survey, maps, measured plans, drawings and sketches, replicas or other traditional and modern technologies;

   b) Recording methodologies should, wherever possible, use non-intrusive techniques and should not cause damage to the object being recorded;

   c) The rationale for the intended scope and the recording method should be clearly stated;

   d) The materials used for compiling the finished record must be archivally stable.

Content of Records

1. Any record should be identified by:

    a) the name of the building, group of buildings or site;

    b) a unique reference number;

    c) the date of compilation of the record;

    d) the name of the recording organisation;

    e) cross-references to related building records and reports, photographic, graphic, textual or bibliographic documentation, archaeological and environmental records.

2. The location and extent of the monument, group of buildings or site must be given accurately; this may be achieved by description, maps, plans or aerial photographs. In rural areas a map reference or triangulation to known points may be the only methods available. In urban areas an address or street reference may be sufficient.

3. New records should note the sources of all information not obtained directly from the monument, group of buildings or site itself.

4. Records should include some or all of the following information:

    a) the type, form and dimensions of the building, monument or site;

    b) the interior and exterior characteristics, as appropriate, of the monument, group of buildings or site;

    c) the nature, quality, cultural, artistic and scientific significance of the heritage and its components and the cultural, artistic and scientific significance of:

    — the materials, constituent parts and construction, decoration, ornament or inscriptions,

    — services, fittings and machinery,

    — ancillary structures, the gardens, landscape and the cultural, topographical and natural features of the site;

    d) the traditional and modern technology and skills used in construction and maintenance;

    e) evidence to establish the date of origin, authorship, ownership, the original design, extent, use and decoration;

    f) evidence to establish the subsequent history of its uses, associated events, structural or decorative alterations, and the impact of human or natural external forces;

    g) the history of management, maintenance and repairs;

    h) representative elements or samples of construction or site materials;

i) an assessment of the current condition of the heritage;

j) an assessment of the visual and functional relationship between the heritage and its setting;

k) an assessment of the conflicts and risks from human or natural causes, and from environmental pollution or adjacent land uses.

5. In considering the different reasons for recording (see Section 1.2 above) different levels of detail will be required. All the above information, even if briefly stated, provides important data for local planning and building control and management. Information in greater detail is generally required for the site or building owner's, manager's or user's purposes for conservation, maintenance and use.

Management, Dissemination and Sharing of Records

1. The original records should be preserved in a safe archive, and the archive's environment must ensure permanence of the information and freedom from decay to recognised international standards.

2. A complete back-up copy of such records should be stored in a separate safe location.

3. Copies of such records should be accessible to the statutory authorities, to concerned professionals and to the public, where appropriate, for the purposes of research, development controls and other administrative and legal processes.

4. Up-dated records should be readily available, if possible on the site, for the purposes of research on the heritage, management, maintenance and disaster relief.

5. The format of the records should be standardised, and records should be indexed wherever possible to facilitate the exchange and retrieval of information at a local, national or international level.

6. The effective assembly, management and distribution of recorded information requires, wherever possible, the understanding and the appropriate use of up-to-date information technology.

7. The location of the records should be made public.

8. A report of the main results of any recording should be disseminated and published, when appropriate.

O.GRA.RO. s.r.l.
ROMA • VICOLO DEI TABACCHI 1
TEL. 5818605 - 5895479 • FAX 5886034